Enlightenment Pie

Healing Through Spiritual Practice

LISA M. GUNSHORE

BALBOA.
PRESS

A DIVISION OF HAY HOUSE

Balboa Press books may be ordered through booksellers or by contacting:

Balboa Press
A Division of Hay House
1663 Liberty Drive
Bloomington, IN 47403
www.balboapress.com
1 (877) 407-4847

Because of the dynamic nature of the Internet, any web addresses or links contained in this book may have changed since publication and may no longer be valid. The views expressed in this work are solely those of the author and do not necessarily reflect the views of the publisher, and the publisher hereby disclaims any responsibility for them.

The author of this book does not dispense medical advice or prescribe the use of any technique as a form of treatment for physical, emotional, or medical problems without the advice of a physician, either directly or indirectly. The intent of the author is only to offer information of a general nature to help you in your quest for emotional and spiritual well-being. In the event you use any of the information in this book for yourself, which is your constitutional right, the author and the publisher assume no responsibility for your actions.

Any people depicted in stock imagery provided by Getty Images are models, and such images are being used for illustrative purposes only. Certain stock imagery © Getty Images.

Print information available on the last page.

ISBN: 978-1-9822-1445-6 (sc)
ISBN: 978-1-9822-1443-2 (hc)
ISBN: 978-1-9822-1444-9 (e)

Library of Congress Control Number: 2018912437

Balboa Press rev. date: 10/25/2018

Dedication

The Recipe

Every good pie begins with a recipe that has been tested over many years until it is just right. The ingredients may change, the measurements may be adjusted; even the filling can be swapped out as the collective palate of your family and friends evolve. The best recipe becomes rooted in family traditions that are passed on from generation to generation. Over time it becomes a part of your history and your family's story. Enlightenment conjures ideas of peace, joy, love and abundance. Enlightenment represents the culmination of love combined with dedication and effort. Enlightenment Pie is a decade of discipline and perseverance required for me to become healthy. We may get burned in the kitchen, but the happiness shared with family and friends is worth the danger. Enlightenment Pie connects the unique story we carry through our lineage with a spiritual practice that, when applied, can bring us to a happier and healthier state.

The tradition of family dessert birthed the idea of Enlightenment Pie. It started as a joke during a meal with my sister and her two young children at a Perkins in a small Colorado town. It has become a tradition with my sister to eat at Perkins when I visit her. Since there isn't one near my home I absolutely love the opportunity. I grew up in rural Iowa where Perkins was a weekly and sometimes daily visit. The familiar smells, floral wallpaper, and vinyl booths conjures memories of home and childhood. On this particular day we went for lunch with my niece and nephew. I had recently returned from Berkeley, California where for the first time I saw His Holiness the Dalai Lama speak. I was sharing with my sister what I had recently discovered about my own spiritual work and enlightenment. There were many jokes passed around the table as I tried to explain enlightenment to my young cohorts. Soon afterward we came to the end of our meal. I promised the kids that we would order pie. Isn't that what Aunts do? My nephew, a very good listener, cracked a joke that it would be 'enlightenment pie'. We all laughed. My niece immediately requested I ask a future partner whether he liked enlightenment pie. I recently divorced and they were on a mission to find a new uncle. My nephew retorted, "he should say yes!" Then my niece very naively said, "tell him... he can eat pie all day long!" My sister and I burst out laughing, all thanks to our dirty minds.

This story reminds me of the lesson to live life with the wisdom of a master and the innocence of a child. If only we could capture that innocence more often, especially when life is most challenging. Spending time with my niece and nephew redirects me to innocence and it's important for me to stay in touch with them to this day. The laughter, jokes, and lightness of Spirit that I feel when we are together replenishes my heart with compassion. The wonderful spirit of the meal filled me with joy for weeks when I thought about that conversation with my sister, niece, and nephew.

This is how 'Enlightenment Pie' began. It combines into loving essence the following: laughter shared amongst family and friends, childlike innocence, family traditions, the promise of new beginnings, the hope of a satisfying ending, and the comforting fullness from a delicious meal. Pie is an indulgent beginning to a lazy Sunday morning or to a young relationship in a booth at Perkins. Pie is the finishing touch of a perfect dinner on a fall night. Combined moments of simplicity and light hold relationships together and give us peace of mind. This harmony is a key to our happiness and the purpose of our work. My hope is for the reader to find this energy, this internal place. The journal within this book will provide tools to begin the journey to better health.

This book is dedicated to the children who have brought an abundance of joy to my life. You remind me there can always be an innocent and creative approach to the growth and constant change that is life. I am passionate about teaching you how to take care of your *Self* so that you may continue to heal generations to come.

Sienna, Joe and Nathan; you have been a special part of my life since I first began the journey of healing.

Drielle, you gave me my first lessons in motherhood for which I am forever grateful.

Maya, Dominic, Brenna and Sadie; you are all part of a wonderful beginning to a whole new chapter of my life.

You are my lights.

You are my inspiration.

Statement of Intent

As a Holistic Health Practitioner and Medical Intuitive I present eating and healthy living options. I suggest nutritional changes based on established resources such as www.candidadiet.org and the mold diet as suggested by Dr. Schoemaker[1]. I am certified in Nutritional Cooking and hold an A.A.S. degree in Culinary Arts and consequently offer sound cooking advice and culinary nutrition information. I help clients incorporate healthy, vitamin and nutrient rich foods into meals. I will teach you, the reader, about phytonutrients and healthy fats. I am neither a medical doctor nor a registered dietician. I will not prescribe, diagnose, or cure any disease or medical issue. While I may suggest nutritional supplements to enhance your healthy lifestyle, I will not prescribe supplements to treat a medical condition. It is very important to have your own team of doctors to support any medical diagnosis or treatment. My counseling and intuitive guidance is meant to support your current medical advice and to enhance your healthy lifestyle overall. This book is intended to be a resource and is not meant to re-create any diet or to offer medical advice. This book shares the knowledge I have gained through research I have done in regard to mold and candida diets, supplementation, and food.

Statement of Belief

I am a fourth generation psychic medium. I was raised Irish Catholic and confirmed in the Catholic Church. In 2010 I converted to Vajrayana Buddhism. It is my belief that God and all Sentient Beings are interconnected. I believe there is a world beyond time and space we may never fully understand as Human Beings, yet we are able to tap into this world through our conscious and unconscious minds. Learning about religion, belief, psychic phenomena, and so on, is ongoing and there is always more to understand. Although I am a Psychic and I understand the many facets of the Occult; I do not identify with Paganism, Wicca

---

[1] Ritchie Shoemaker, M. D., is a recognized leader in patient care, research and education pioneer in the field of biotoxin related illness. http://www.survivingmold.com/about/ritchie-shoemaker-m-d

or other Occult religions. I currently practice Vajrayana Buddhism, and the Middle Way is what I try to incorporate in my daily life. I have an appreciation for my Catholic upbringing and the family values I learned growing up. I respect all religions as they have something to offer the open mind. My belief is that all things are an interconnected web of Divine energy.

Preface

The Whirlwind (December 2010 – March 2011)

Crawling on my hands and knees, I barely made it through my mother's front door and into her spare bathroom. My mind was racing as I projectile vomited the lunch I had eaten in the car on my drive from Denver to Cedar Rapids. My head felt swollen and foggy. A migraine that enveloped my sinuses, mouth, and forehead had me spinning and aching. My ears were ringing incessantly. My vision by now was blurred, and I could barely stand the light in the room. Bizarre prisms were flashing in my left eye whether it was open or closed. None of this had ever happened to me before. I laid on my mother's bathroom floor unable to function, wondering, *"what in the world has happened to me?"*

I was able to stop vomiting and made my way into her spare bedroom. I crawled under the covers. A thousand pictures cycled in my mind and I was unable to stop them. I felt unbelievably strange. A sadness surrounded my head and mind like a heavy fog. I began to cry. I laid in bed while my mom held me. I wanted my life to end, as I had experienced unexplained symptoms for over three months. This was the first moment in my life where I distinctly felt like I just wanted out of this mess. My body was shaking and my anxiety was high. My mom gave me half a Valium and held me while my body calmed down. I looked up at my mom and told her, "Mom. If I die tonight, I want you to know that I love you." After the effects of the Valium washed over me, I fell into a deep sleep. It was the first night in two months that I slept through the night. Being home with my mom meant I was able to let go. I had been so sick and had been managing my condition all alone. I was afraid to sleep, scared that I would not wake up.

The incident above occurred in January of 2011. I found out several months later that, in actuality, my symptoms and health issues could be traced back to a weak immune system I've had since birth. Ironically, as a child, my life seemed to be free of major health issues. Of course, many smaller problems were observed as exclusive maladies, and no pattern was ever established. In 2011, I was working in Fashion Retail as a General Manager in my early 30's and had a successful career to that point. On the weekends I was out socializing with friends and acquaintances. I had lost 50 pounds since my divorce two years earlier and was looking and feeling better than I had in a long time. I was also conducting psychic readings for a few hours each week and had built a global clientele. All seemed well with my current environment.

One night I met a close friend at a restaurant known for its pizza and large beer selection. We had been working on a "Beer Tour" for several weeks and met that night to complete their Winterfest tour for a free t-shirt. We had what I considered "a grand old time!" The conversation was largely nonsensical, and I hadn't laughed so hard in a long time. The evening out was light-hearted, however, by the time I arrived home I noticed something inside my lower lip. I was talking on my cell phone with another one of my friends and suddenly realized that a white bump was forming inside my mouth. I became upset as I wondered... a canker sore?!? I then grew extremely frustrated. Upon waking the next morning the sore had multiplied from one to two. I was now feeling fatigued and nauseous, as if I was being struck by a terrible virus.

Up to this point in my life, I rarely sought medical attention. However, I had a bad case of pneumonia in November of 2010 that caused me to faint at work. I was given a shot of penicillin in my ass(!) to avoid hospitalization and consequently missed two weeks of work. It was because of that incident with pneumonia that I thought I had better check in with a doctor. After the doctor checked the sores in my mouth, he told me that I had a virus and should go home to rest. After two days of little to no activity, the sores had spread throughout my entire mouth. I was in a great deal of pain and by now incredibly exhausted. Throughout this physical challenge, I managed to work my shifts. After another exhausting retail shift I left work, took some Nyquil, and slept all night and the following day. The morning after my marathon sleep session, I was still searching for a cure to the sores in my mouth. At the recommendation of a friend who works for an ENT, I visited an Otolaryngologist who diagnosed me with canker sores and prescribed steroids and viral medication.

After taking this new medication for two days I began to feel better. My energy was returning and I was feeling vibrant again. My mouth was beginning to heal and I thought life was returning to its normal state. I went to brunch with a friend and was feeling motivated and ready to return to my schedule until the unexpected occurred. I barely made it home from brunch before I was sick again. My whole body crashed. I suddenly became very fatigued and nauseous, again. I decided I had better lay down and rest in my apartment. By that night my entire body felt heavy and beyond anything I had experienced prior. I had no energy and I felt my gums inside my mouth swelling all around my teeth. Not only was my mouth in a great deal of pain, but the steroids I had been prescribed were making me literally crazy. I found myself up at three o'clock in the morning with sweats and paranoia. I was so hot that I yanked my window open in the dead of winter. I felt like I might jump out of my skin. I remember wondering, "is this what it felt like to turn into a werewolf?" I suddenly felt like I had lost control of my mind. While I laid in bed a thousand pictures ran through my mind so quickly I could hardly acknowledge them; childhood memories, scenes from old soap operas, fleeting moments of recent occurrences. It was so bizarre and scary. Was I going to die? Was this my life flashing before my eyes? My nervous system was reacting in a very odd way and I felt it 'tweaking'. I had no experience with anything like this before. My body was shaking violently as though an earthquake was trapped inside of me. Most frightening was that I didn't understand any of it. After I stood at my apartment window for what seemed like an eternity, I grabbed my rosary and the Kuan Yin[2] statue I had on my altar and prayed to the angels and my spirit guides to please help me make it through the night. I thought, "if I wake up tomorrow, then I am meant to live".

---

[2] Kuan Yin is the female form of Avalokitesvara in Tibetan Buddhism; the female Boddhisattva of Compassion.

Introduction (January 2006 – December 2008)

I want to begin by expressing my great gratitude to all the incredible teachers and healers that have blessed my life and countless others. We are very fortunate to live in a time full of living teachers willing to share and embody the teachings of Enlightened Beings. It is through these teachings, passed down through various lineages, that have taught me how to heal myself. Whether it has been emotional or physical crises, I have been able to recover and, in some instances, move beyond limitations into a new realm.

I may look and act differently from people who communicate with spiritual intention. I am just a simple woman. I don't speak in hushed, reverent tones. A client tells me I sound more like a cheerleader on the phone than a Delphic oracle. I love fashion, art, and food. On the surface I may appear as a middle-aged woman who loves a beautiful pair of heels, but inside I am a fourth generation practicing psychic medium[3] with plenty of spiritual experiences to share. Psychic gifts run through the women of my family; my mother reads Tarot cards and has prophetic dreams. Her mother worked with animal totems and herbal medicines. Her mother was a trance channel and automatic wrote poetry and divine messages until her death at 98. It's possible and likely that the psychic gifts extend beyond those four generations. I recently learned that my father's side of the family have also experienced psychic phenomena. In

---

[3] A Medium is the practice of certain people—known as mediums—to purportedly mediate communication between spirits of the dead and living human beings. There are different types of mediumship including spirit channeling, and Ouija.

an effort to understand psychic events I have seen and felt since I was a young child, and consequently what to do with the information given, I have been searching for answers of a spiritual nature most of my life.

When I was a small child I carried a lot of fear. I was afraid of the dark. I was afraid of being in my bedroom alone at night. From the doorway of my bedroom I would run in a panic to my bed. I would jump onto my bed and tuck my feet under the covers. It appeared silly. I didn't want anything to 'get me'. I felt the presence of energies; some I couldn't see and others were shadows of people. For many years I saw a man in blue overalls. He would stand in the doorway of my room watching me. He had silver hair and a bushy mustache. In retrospect, I feel he was protecting me in some way. But at the time I felt incredibly scared of him. Who was he? I wanted an answer to this question and started reading books on spirituality and the Occult. In one book I read how to facilitate a séance. I followed the directions and spent an entire afternoon trying to connect with the shadows that lingered near me. I often felt different from everyone else. I felt misunderstood and unable to share what I felt or saw even though I wanted the same things. I had crushes on boys in high school and worked hard to become a cheerleader. I sang in church choir and loved acting in school plays. I was very creative and had a desire to write endlessly. Still, each night, I ran to my bed and hid under the covers.

Researching spirituality and experimenting with the esoteric has been a recurring theme throughout my life. I comfortably operated in the mundane with respect to careers, relationships, and so on. Behind the scenes I was reading about meditation, different religions and analytical psychology. There was a drive inside of me to know more. I wanted to feel connected to innate abilities that existed since childhood. My research on the spiritual realms led me to universal teachings about happiness and manifestation. At first, I struggled with those teachings. It was hard to understand that happiness comes from within. The discontent I felt was really of my own doing. Happiness does not come from any 'thing' or any one person. Ever since I first became aware of these Truths, it has been a delicate balance between the trappings of my life and my quest for spiritual attainment. My current understanding is that 'letting go' is about accepting the circumstances of your life exactly as they exist today. By doing so you can allow more abundance and fullness into your life. When you let go you can be happy with your existence right now in the present moment.

I have been challenged for nearly forty years with chronic illness and co-dependency. I repeatedly sought something or someone to fill me up and to make me feel content. For years I depended on external validation, trusted dishonest people, and operated without functional boundaries. This left me exhausted. From that exhaustion came an awakening that would change the course of my life. The process of awakening was so subtle I was often unaware of its impact. Suddenly my life would be different, change again, and yet again. This constant shifting may have looked unstable to an observer. But to me it was everything I needed to become who I am today. I am in recovery today. I feel strength within myself. I still face obstacles every day, but I am confident I am headed in the right direction. I have always known I would share my story, but it wasn't until now that I really knew what story to share. I know now that I must have courage to speak the truth and to state the challenges I have faced and how I came to heal. I do this for everyone facing similar struggles. I speak on behalf of all my clients I've worked with for over 10 years who have felt the same pain. I have developed a system I want to share with you, with specific process steps to recover from what seems like an endless pattern of struggle with health and discontent.

I was unsure how to begin the story of my spirituality and its link to my health. At first, I thought this all started 10 years ago when I started reading people as a professional psychic[4]. With deeper analysis I thought it started when I was 5 years old and had my tonsils removed. I was

---

[4] A psychic is someone who embodies or exhibits phenomena such as; precognition, telepathy, extra-sensory perception, and Clair Senses. Clair Senses in psychic terms are translated: clairvoyance, clairaudience, clairsentience, clairscent, clairtangency, and clairgustance.
Clairvoyance - (from French clair meaning "clear" and voyance meaning "vision") is the alleged ability to gain information about an object, person, location or physical event through extrasensory perception.

chronically sick as a young child with tonsillitis and strep. Did it start when I was born? Maybe when I chose to be born? Was it in the last life? In order for me to understand the order in which to share my story, I needed to research my own life. During that research a miraculous thing occurred. I was able to see my patterns of behavior that created drama and resulted in destructive emotions[5]. I also noticed a clear set of steps that I followed each time I overcame a destructive pattern with my health or my emotions. I decided to formulate these process steps and establish a clear system for healing. This book is the culmination of years of research and profound moments of awakening. It gives me great joy to share with you the system, the process steps, and the resources that have brought me into a balanced state of healing.

This book is not for the light-hearted. This is for Seekers who have at least begun their spiritual journey. This is for those of you who are interested in or studying Buddhism or Yoga philosophies and who

---

Clairaudience - (clear hearing) the supposed faculty of perceiving, as if by hearing, what is inaudible.

Clairsentience - (clear feeling) Quite possibly the most under-estimated psychic gift, is the ability to feel strongly and sense the emotions and feelings of people, animals, spirits, and places around them. You can feel emotions of others both in your heart and in your body; you can likely feel spirits around you.

Clairtangency - Psychometry, or Clairtangency (clear touching), is the ability to sense information by touch. Usually, this is applied to an inanimate object, such as a piece of jewelry, clothing or even a motor vehicle. The word 'psychometry' literally means 'measuring the soul' and was coined by Joseph Rodes Buchanan in 1842.

Clairgustance - The paranormal ability to taste a substance without putting anything in one's mouth. It is claimed the those who possess this ability are able to perceive the essence of a substance from the spiritual or ethereal realms through taste.

Psychometry – divination of facts concerning an object or its owner through contact with or proximity to the object. First Known Use: circa 1842

Telepathy – communication from one mind to another by extrasensory means.

Precognition – knowledge of a future event or situation, especially through extrasensory means

[5] Destructive Emotions in Buddhism are often called *kleshas*; defilements that disturb the equilibrium of your mind. Examples of destructive emotions are; hatred, jealousy, greed etc.

are ready to go head first into meditation and journaling practices. You must be determined to maintain an open mind throughout this effort. In order to complete the defined activities, you need to be brave enough to look at the shadow aspects of yourself. You must be willing to be honest with yourself. William Shakespeare wrote, "This thing of darkness I acknowledge mine." And Carl Jung[6] was quoted; "We have met the enemy and he is us." This book is not only a collection of stories about my own health challenges, but also a system that will enable you to look within at your own dysfunction and help you to purify that darkness into light.

Journal Entry Fall 2010

As I sit here in the quiet of the midnight hours my thoughts are filled with words. The philosophy of great masters such as Osho[7] and Lao Tzu[8]; of Buddha himself. Sometimes when all the world has gone quiet– so too can our minds. The empty space is then filled with Spirit who tells us exactly what to do. Spirit speaks to me. She tells me of my heart and its deepest longings to be free from the pain of the world as it is known to man. My heart weeps but not in sadness; instead she weeps for all those who cannot see the maya before them. She calls to the seekers lost in the trance of the world, the mundane. How will they find their way out? How will they awaken from their slumber known as unconsciousness? For some the awakening will be brutal. A jolt from the unknown manifested as a car accident or a job loss or some unforeseen trauma. For others it will be subtler. They will sense that they are missing something. Their inner knowing will be calling them home. And they will begin to look for home – all of them. They will seek it from teachers, masters and books. They will find it in a song or in the wind. Home will forever call them, and they will find their way there. Like the scent of your mother's perfume or of your grandfather's wool; it will fill up your senses with nostalgic memories

---

[6] Carl Jung was the founder of analytical psychology. His book; *Memories, Dreams Reflections,* has been an integral part in my journey of understanding. I highly recommend this book.

[7] Osho was known as a controversial Guru and modern-day philosopher. For more information go to www.osho.com.

[8] Lao Tzu was the founder of Taoism.

of a place so familiar and yet it will remain nameless. Our hearts will fill up with this nostalgic energy bringing us further from our slumber and closer to the light. Taking them on the 'magic' school bus into the unknown, into the space of the heart, into pure consciousness. This space known to me in this late hour as 'home'.

How does one awaken? When we drift through the endless sea of sleep; how do we then decide to step onto land? A traumatic experience jolts some of us upright; others experience fear as though being forced through small holes in a grater of cheese. Many have a 'knowing' that there is something greater than themselves and a small nudge is all that is needed to take you from the numbing slumber. I remember the day I came awake. On that day the clouds hung low in the sky. Although the seasons were beginning to change it felt much like the many winter days before it.

I was raised in the Catholic church. My brother and I went to Catechism and I sang in the church choir. My parents weren't strict Catholics, still, we did attend church most Sundays. My favorite part of church was going out to breakfast afterwards. Father Lenoch was our priest. He was a small, elderly man who had a great sense of humor and often shared a comic during his Sunday Sermon. As a teenager, I was confused about where I stood in my spiritual beliefs. I liked church and the idea of it. There were angels and prayers and the lyrics in each song spoke to me. But I was a psychic. I saw things and felt things that were out of the ordinary. I didn't understand how that fit in to my Catholic upbringing.

We didn't talk about it as a family, but my parents were open to the idea of psychic phenomena, mysticism and the Esoteric. They knew I had abilities and they also knew I had some bizarre experiences. My mom also encountered prophetic dreams and strange phenomena. In my early 20's I had been obsessively focused on the Esoteric. I read Tarot cards and began to practice meditation. When I married at 25 I stopped engaging with spirituality. I'm not sure why. I was caught up in my career and I had a step-daughter that required a great deal of time and effort to raise and I had to juggle finances and responsibilities to keep us afloat. I shut off the part of me that was connected to Spirit. At this point I hadn't said a prayer or given a thought to my spiritual gifts locked deep inside me for over 10 years. With a longing for answers and nowhere else to turn, I was ready to turn back to God.

A combination of guilt, trauma, and grief pushed me to open myself to God. The higher power that was separated from my life now reconnected. Through choices and circumstances, I still work to understand, I lost a child. My loss was profound. It left me struggling to find meaning in my life. I was wrestling with my grief. I felt guilt at my relief that I was not going to be tied to a toxic relationship with a child, and heartbroken that I was not going to have the baby. The emotions were confusing and disrupting any focus I had on other aspects of my life. I found myself overweight. The heaviness I felt was both the literal weight I gained as well as the sadness within my heart. As far back as I could remember I lived with subtle but growing discontent and my recent experiences only expanded it. The discontent weighed on me as an abused elephant might sit on its trainer.

I had a home in a rural area outside of Castle Rock, CO, where the houses were spaced well apart from one another. At the edge of our neighborhood there was trail that led to a cliff overlooking nearby Franktown. It provided a beautiful view. I walked this trail every once in a while with my dog. Today I walked farther than normal with my basset hound Max and stared down at the small town below. I cried. A man and a woman walked past with their dog. I paid no mind to their glances as my tear-stained face gave it all away. I just asked, *"What am I supposed to do?"* I heard a voice from the Heavens. I am certain it was a higher being. His loud booming voice rolled through my head like thunder. *"Go home and get your cards."* These words rang through my ears. My cards. I hadn't thought of those in what seemed like years. Without another thought I began to run home, my basset hound in tow. Looking back, I imagine we must have looked a bit ridiculous—a round, tearstained woman running with her pudgy basset hound.

When we made it home I began to tear through boxes until I came across my deck of Tarot Cards. They were worn from my frequent and enthusiastic use in the first years I had owned them. I had not touched them for 10 years. In fact, my now ex-husband did not even know I read them. Since I married I had not thrown a card, used my intuitive senses or had felt connected to the spirit realm. Because of my fears and a need to be 'asleep' for a time I had shut down my gifts and abilities. I had become focused on the mundane – work, money and marriage. I opened the box and pulled out my deck. I began to throw the cards. The symbols were age old and now they lay staring back at me. I remembered the images and their divine meanings, likely from other lifetimes. I felt a longing from deep inside well up. I knew it was time to do something about what I was feeling. I knew my gifts that had been locked away needed to be shared with the outside world. No matter how many times I shuffled those cards and laid them out they told me it was time to help others.

I went downstairs and told my husband I was a psychic. He really didn't know what to say. I told him it was time for me to start using my gifts to help people. He still didn't know what to say. That moment, from that day on the trail, had changed the trajectory of my life. After years of 'tuning out', I began to 'tune in'. I opened myself back up to the realm of Spirit, to God. In doing so, I was really opening myself back up to me, to my authentic being, to the Spirit of God that lies within.

'Life is a series of cycles and a time of rebirth is indicated for you. This may mean a new phase in a relationship, the germination of a fresh idea or the development of qualities in you like laughter, light or hope. It may herald a total change. Do not be afraid to let go of the familiar, for the new cannot enter until the old and outworn has departed. Your angel guidance is to accept the new for it will be welcome when it arrives. Birth is a vulnerable time. The fragile life force needs to be protected and nurtured within you. Ask the angels to guide the new beginnings in your life safely to maturity.'

Diana Cooper Angels of Light[9]

Planting the Seed

In Buddhism they teach that we all have the seed of awakening inside of us.

The 'Buddha Nature' or the idea that we all possess a sacred nature and/or an innate luminous mind that is the basis to become a Buddha. It is through cultivation of that seed that you can develop this clear light mind and move ever closer to awakening.

For me, I think of it as a flower opening. You first plant the seed and then the seed begins to grow. The more you feed it; the more it grows. Then there's this moment in your life when the flower begins to blossom. The essence of awakening suddenly comes alive and the layers of the petals open farther and farther. For me, that day that I pulled out my Tarot cards, was the day my seed began to sprout. It has continued to expand and grow more and more each day since then and in ways I never expected or could have even began to sense more than a decade ago.

It was March of 2006 that I started re-learning how to read Tarot cards. I read countless books and took tests to become a Certified Professional Tarot Reader (CPTR) with the Tarot Certification Board of America. I made business cards and set up an open house on July 11, 2006 for my friends to come and test me out. It was a huge success and word of mouth began spreading. By the fall of that year I was reading clients 5 hours or more a week in addition to my full-time job. I also began attending the Psychic Institute in Boulder, CO[10] to study clairvoyance

---

[9] Diana Cooper is a contemporary artist who created a deck of cards called; *Angels of Light*. To view this deck go to https://www.amazon.com/Angels-Light-Cards -Pocket-Cooper/dp/1844091716.

[10] Psychic Horizons Center is in Boulder, CO https://www.psychichorizonscenter. org/; if you are interested in learning more about this program and/or are not able to afford this program I highly recommend *You Are Psychic* by Debra Lynne Katz. It is an excellent book for developing your clairvoyant abilities. To purchase https:// www.amazon.com/You-Are-Psychic-Clairvoyant-Reading/dp/0989094170.

and energy healing. I couldn't soak up enough of the information I was receiving! While you may not feel like you are accomplishing much going to a meditation class or visiting a healer, you are actually creating major shifts in your life whether you acknowledge it or not. The journey of healing and of attainment is about knowledge. The Dalai Lama, who I discovered to be my Guru in 2009, speaks of the importance of continued education in almost every talk he gives.

His Holiness said recently that you cannot understand the nature of reality or the nature of mind without learning science and the ways of the world.

We forget this, because society teaches us that our time to learn ends when we finish high school, or college, or a graduate program. But the more you learn about the workings of energy, the world, science and spirituality, the greater understanding you will have about yourself. This path can lead to powerful healing within your being and your very nature.

After a year of study, I left my retail career behind to be a psychic and healer. Business was good, and I had clients all over the country. But, at the same time, I desperately needed to heal myself. I was struggling with key issues that I would not understand until later. I hadn't had my menstrual cycle for nearly two years. Even though I was married at the time I had no desire to be sexually active. My base and sacral chakras[11] were completely shut down. I was constantly sick. I had chronic sinus and ear infections most of my life and was exhausted all the time. I recall scheduled readings where I could barely get out of bed to conduct the sessions. The energy issues would come and go. The crazy thing is that I really didn't think anything of my issues at the time. Yet it had everything to do with serious health issues that I would only uncover years later. Now writing this all down, I am amazed at how many things I believed I had to tolerate. I had convinced myself the problems were

---

[11] Chakras are recognized energy centers in the body. Chakra is a sanskrit word that translates into wheel. There are seven major chakras but there are 114 recognized chakras in the body.

not really a big deal when they were actually major signs that my health was in continual decline.

Not only did I have all these physical challenges, I also had to sort out emotional issues. In my first year as a professional psychic I was very successful, partially because I had unconsciously built a practice based on a foundation of codependency. I allowed clients to text and call me day and night. Some clients became "friends" and would suddenly get angry or disappear when they didn't get the immediate attention they craved. I seemed to disappoint all sorts of people during this time. In my mind, I wasn't able to embody the help they wanted. It is a challenge to work in the spiritual realm because many people have expectations that you are always living your own clean and spiritual life. I imagine clients have an image of the healing community sitting in a cave meditating every morning. But of course, that is far from reality. I was a normal person in my daily habits, a human being going about her day, and coincidentally I was operating from my own place of dysfunction. I remember the first time I saw the Dalai Lama speak and he said he was 'a simple monk'. He told a story of his jealousy of the relationship between his teacher and a bird. I remember it came as a relief to me, hearing him talk of his own humanness, jealousy, and anger.[12]

We are all human.

In that first year my seed had begun to sprout from the ground, but it was in the summer of 2008 that it finally started to blossom. I had reached out to a healer in the Bahamas. I had been told she could access the Akashic records and that her healings and readings were incredible. I decided to schedule an alignment with her. I had no idea what would open up when I did this. Since we first met, Julie has become my most sacred teacher, colleague, and guide over the past ten years.[13] The chain of events that have unfolded since are so profound that I shiver with goosebumps and gratitude in this very moment. I shiver because I am

---

[12] Dalai Lama sharing his bird story. https://youtu.be/qd2OAUQq5AE
[13] Julie Hoyle is an author, artist and personal growth teacher. www. truealignment.org

able to look back on the last decade and see the connections to every step of the path that has unfolded since that time. My alignment revealed a great deal to me. Much of it I didn't understand or comprehend the depth until now. I was told that my purpose was to move into a state of complete health and balance in order to serve as a bridge to connect seekers to unseen realms. The meaning and magnitude of that purpose now resonates in every layer of my life experiences. After the alignment and phone session with Julie I found myself opening a new door on my spiritual path. Until this point I was studying the Occult and reading about meditation and divination. The alignment energy firmly placed me on a new path focused on enlightenment and unity consciousness.

I had an intense lucid dream[14] following the alignment in which Nityananda[15] came to me. He was floating above my prostrate body and began drawing patterns over my chakras. I saw my Chakras open and colors began to pour out of me. When I awoke from this potent experience I felt very strange with an openness I had not felt before. I wrote my new-found teacher and to my surprise discovered this experience was incredibly purposeful. I had received Shaktipat initiation.

Shaktipat refers in Hinduism to the conferring of spiritual "energy" upon one person by another.

It is an opening of energy, more specifically the opening of the Kundalini[16]. This initiation is an act of Grace as defined by Siddha Yoga teachings. Grace indeed! This marked the beginning of a journey of self-discovery and healing that has completely changed my nature from my physical form to my own genetic structures. Two days later I had my period for the first time in two years. I knew I could no longer hide from the awareness that showed me a path to healing. It was finally

---

[14] Lucid dreaming is where you, the dreamer, is aware you are having a dream. Tayria Ward is a depth psychologist and dream analyst out of North Carolina. She is an excellent resource for dream work; http://tayriaward.com/
[15] Baghawan Nityananda is an Indian Guru and Hindu Saint.
[16] Kundalini is a Sanskrit word that refers to the primal energy that begins at the base of the spine.

time to make big changes in my life to become happy. It is important to understand I mistakenly thought my focus was to become content and not to become healthy. I was under an illusion that my physical health was fine, and ending my relationship was all I needed to get my life on track. It is only now that I grasp the power of strong physical health and its important connection to both spiritual and emotional health. Healing one's whole self is what enables happiness to arise. Healing and happiness are conjoined; you cannot have one without the other.

When I opened my office doors as a psychic and healer on July 11, 2006, I distractedly felt it was my calling to heal others. What I learned over the next decade was that this calling was to heal myself. It was through the mirror of my clients and incredibly gifted healers and psychics that have supported me on the way that I was able to see and break many of my own destructive behavioral patterns. A willingness to initiate inner work, or self-inquiry practice, will help heal and burn through your karma. You must be brave. There were many times I wanted to quit, but something deep inside trusted that the Universe will continue to support me and show me the way. That trust is tantamount to healing yourself because without it you may slow, stop, or even reverse your progress. My book will carry you through the process, but you must bring faith and courage with you on this journey.

I ended my marriage in November 2008 and finalized the divorce in April 2009. After my divorce I found myself with a lot of time to contemplate all that had been revealed through my recent hardships. Life since then up until today has been filled with various measures of love, happiness, anger, and sadness. I have had beautiful friends and challenging relationships. I have loved deeply; regretted as deeply and moved forward one small step at a time. I know I have not been here long in comparison to some. To others I may have already been here forever. Again, I have just been. And in 'being' here I have learned a great deal about life. I have read philosophy, studied the Spirit, come to understand how to work a computer and finally learned to text. It has brought me here. To the place I now stand. The present. And what does the present have to offer? Everything? Nothing? The present is…just That. The present, the All. The All There Is. This moment contains everything. It contains every thought; every memory of the past and every idea for the future. The 'Now' holds the key to every great philosophy and every great truth. It took me thirty plus years, ten jobs, five relationships, four family divorces (including my own), losing pets, buying a home and then losing it, declaring bankruptcy, one car accident, leaving my job in search of my spiritual self (only to return to work two years later), and living the life of the 'proverbial fool' to reach the conclusion that nothing really matters, nothing really exists, we are all One, the present moment is All There Is and that Love is the key to finding yourself and God.

We all embark on our own unique journeys, and every day that we wake up we must pack our bags for the road ahead. We manifest where we are headed. We make decisions regarding the choices we see in front of us. Sometimes those choices are free from attachments and other times we feel they are forced and tied to the outcomes. These are the journeys of our souls. Where are we headed? A Buddhist would say it is not about the destination. The past is gone, and the future is not yet. All we have is this moment, right now. In a world full of wonderment and in a career where many wants to know the future; I see now why I get stuck there myself. Is everything written in the stars? Do we make choices or are they made for us? If so, who makes them? Is it God? Is there a God? And the questions go on and on.

I believe that we create our own lives. I am not a fatalist. Many people that I speak with believe they are stuck or meant to live a life of pain and misery. The truth that I have experienced through my own trials is that you can change course through determination and hard work. I want to stress that throughout the process of growth and change, choices can become challenging and the stakes may increase. Discipline and focus are critical, but you can overcome your setbacks. As before, we will be presented choices to allow our souls the opportunity of freedom. Each choice can move you closer to healing, or further down a destructive path. Each choice is an opportunity for learning, and even poor choices can result in growth. In the present moment, you can choose healing regardless of your past. No matter where we go; no matter how difficult or easy, we still move forward. To learn and to evolve is our soul's purpose.

I began writing Enlightenment Pie in 2011 after a full recovery from a near death health experience. Since then I've been in very different spaces and on very different journeys each time I sat to write. I was very focused on Buddhism in Boulder, CO. I struggled with toxic relationships. I very recently edited this book with my future husband in a house full of four young children. All throughout these years I met the Dalai Lama twice and nearly died on two separate occasions. These written words come from my own truth; I'm sharing my most intense moments of awareness that were poignant to my own healing process.

My nephew's unintended joke drew immediate parallels between some of my spiritual experiences and my culinary education. I had an epiphany that life was like a finished pie. We have a foundation, or a crust and we have different flavors that fill us up. Since then, this rough concept has morphed into something more regimented. Enlightenment Pie is about a relationship with food and health, and how this relationship goes hand in hand with Spirit and baggage carried in this lifetime. Childhood and family are some of the ingredients presented in the healing process. Yogi Bhajan introduced Kundalini yoga to the U.S. and said, "Spiritual practice benefits seven generations before and seven generations after. So know that you not only to this for yourself, but for your ancestors and those who follow." It requires great effort to overcome behavior patterns and even genetics. Peeling back these layers of baggage leads to a blossoming of the authentic Self.

My hope is that there are pieces and parts of my health challenges that connect to pieces and parts of yours. I will do my best to explain the process while holding the depth of the universal teachings and yet applies to the world we live in today. The connection we make with each other and with the information can help us all to heal, better understand ourselves and most importantly, apply the teachings to our everyday struggles of life.

Reader Intention

For those who are searching for Truth beyond the mundane, beyond Samsara[17].

For those who have run out of hope and are searching for the light.

For those who are hungry for knowledge, wisdom and truth.

For those whose souls have committed to a greater calling.

For those who wish to serve the greater good and humanity.

For the warriors[18] who are willing to confront their obstacles and fears head on.

For those who have lost trust in the system and are looking for inner peace, depth, knowledge and understanding.

And So It Is.

---

[17] Samsara is the cycle of death and rebirth to which life in the material world is bound.

[18] Warrior here is defined by *Shambhala: The Sacred Path of the Warrior* written by Chogyam Trunpa Rinpoche. To purchase https://www.amazon.com/dp/B00HEN3JHW/ref=dp-kindle-redirect?_encoding=UTF8&btkr=1

Objective

Living in Vitality

It seems everywhere we look these days; we see more and more people carrying weight. To someone on the outside they may only see the unhealthy side effects of poor diet and pass judgements on the person's ability to care for themselves. What may not be seen is the deep layers of emotional baggage that this person is carrying and their lack of Self Love that ultimately affects their choices when caring or ultimately 'not caring' for themselves. The baggage is really layering that we have acquired throughout this lifetime and others and it has manifested into; physical weight that we carry in our bodies, emotional weight, and spiritual weight in the form of karma.

The purpose of this book is to teach you how to release this weight from your Spirit, mind and body. I have learned from my own experience that to truly 'lose weight' we must complete the inner work in ALL aspects of our lives. By looking at those difficult pieces of ourselves that is our weight; we bring to the surface many destructive emotions. By working through these emotions and facing them - rather than 'stuffing them away'; we are able to overcome this weight once and for all. This book is not really about changing your diet but instead transforming all aspects of your Self and changing your life!

In this book you will learn in depth how to apply the four steps of this process of purification:

1. Become aware – Practice mindfulness. Learn how to be mindful of both your physical body and your emotional body in relation to your food choices and your weight. Become clear about how your Spiritual body and your Karma is affecting your weight and overall health. Learn basic practices to help you move through your inner work with ease and apply them in your daily life. Begin to build a relationship with your physical body and be able to listen and understand its needs.
2. Become wise – Learn how to utilize journaling and self-inquiry to find out as much information as you can about your body and yourself. Learn the basics of mold, candida and folate diet and how to begin the process of managing your food allergies.
3. Practice. Learn how to practice mindfulness and meditation and how to incorporate it into your daily life. Practice self-inquiry through the exercises in the book.
4. TRUST – Faith is the most important piece. You have to trust in yourself and in the Divine. You have to trust that you are always safe in the hands of Spirit. In this journal I share my journey of Trust.

Contents

ENLIGHTENMENT PIE
PURIFY. ENERGIZE. HEAL

Become Aware | Become Wise | Practice | Trust

बाधी:

1

Candida

I could barely make it to work. Every time I tried to work or eat or sleep; I couldn't. I was too scared to sleep. I was afraid I would not wake up. When I ate my mouth and gums would swell and I would feel nauseous. I didn't know what was happening with me. I had been to the emergency room where they found nothing wrong with me. I continued to have extreme anxiety, nervousness, paranoia, nausea, headaches, pain in my mouth. In an effort to get to the root of my mouth issue I went to the dentist. She discovered a severe periodontal infection and I was anxiously awaiting her removing it. She said that I most likely had had this infection for 5 or more years and that it was affecting my immune system in a serious way. She assured me that once it was removed I would feel so much better. Had I really not taken care of myself to the point of a severe infection? After multiple doctor visits to various specialists I was starting to see a pattern that I lacked self-care. And what I thought was overall fine health simply wasn't. I had let so much of my health go thinking this was just how I was. Instead of questioning the subtle changes in my health I just adjusted to it. I didn't seem to think I could change it or needed to. My gums often bled after I brushed my teeth. That was my norm and I hadn't even given thought to the fact that it was totally not normal and a sign of infection.

As soon as I found out I had this infection in my gums I was anxious as hell to get it out of me. It was absolute stress each and every moment waiting in pain for the appointment to arrive. After waiting with much anticipation, I finally was able to have the infection removed. It took the dentist two appointments and almost 8 hours total to remove the infection from my gums. I think the worst part was after the first appointment when only half of my mouth was healthy again. The swelling was gone almost immediately from my gums and the dentist was right; I felt much better. I thought this was it! I have my answer and after my second appointment I thought as soon as this heals I am going to feel great.

I returned to work feeling like I was finally healing. My energy was slowly coming back, and I was able to eat again with my mouth no longer in pain. At this time, it had been a full month since I had gotten so ill and I was hopeful that there was light at the end of the tunnel. The roof of my mouth still would swell up and had a strange pain from time to time, but it would come and go. Being a psychic, I had been looking at my cards through this entire event to try and diagnose myself. I was bothered as my cards continued to say that something was wrong. A couple of my close friends who are also psychic felt there was a condition not yet treated as well. I was also stuck in a very negative mind pattern. The anxiety and panic, in addition to my health, had been running me ragged. I didn't feel like myself, nor did I feel like I had any control or connection over my mind.

It was now week 5 and a beautiful afternoon in February. I grabbed Wendy's on my way down to work. It was an hour drive and I was so happy to be feeling hungry that I celebrated with my favorite cheeseburger. I hadn't had a diet coke for a few weeks because I had been so unwell and got a large one to get my energy rev'd for the day. As a retail manager I was drinking an average of 6 or more diet cokes a day. It was very unusual to go without, but I had been so sick it sounded terrible. It was also very usual for me to get fast food. I had all my favorites. I thought I could eat anything. I had never had any reactions to food and because of my culinary degree was a total foodie. I loved to eat! Of course, food was a huge problem silently lurking in my body. At the time I was a size 12 and happy to be that because I was a size 20 when I got divorced. But why was that size good enough for me? Did

I really think it was fine to still be overweight and eat cheeseburgers? Yep I did.

By the time I got to work I was feeling better. Finally! I was going to get well again and be able to move forward. It had been a long month. The snow, the illness and the darkness were getting the best of me. In fact, the darkness had become a real issue. It seemed like when the clouds were covering the sun and it was dark and wintery I felt miserable. I almost felt overtaken by depression. That was very odd because I often liked the winter weather and it wasn't like me to feel so closed in when the clouds were in the sky. At the time though this bright sunny day was just what I needed. After a couple of hours getting back in the swing of things at my store I stepped back into my office to check the multitude of emails that had accrued in my absence.

Suddenly my hands began to shake, and I felt very strange. My body was reacting to something…it felt like low blood sugar. That shaky feeling where your whole-body tremors because you don't have enough food in your system. But I had eaten lunch? The feeling got worse and to top it off my anxiety went from bad to worse. I found myself standing in the middle of my store in a panic attack. Shaking, nervous and not feeling right I took a break and went next door to try to eat some soup. I sat and ate a bowl of soup while calling my mom in panic. I really didn't know what was wrong? I was so frustrated. What the hell was happening to me? After trying to get it under control, and failing, I ended up going to the emergency room for the second time to figure it out. By the time they got me into a hospital room, my pupils were dilated, my entire body had tremors and I had terrible cotton-mouth. They immediately put me on fluids and ran blood work. My dear friend met me at the hospital and determined that it was like I was overdosing on something. The only thing I could think of was this immune booster tea I had been drinking. Both times I had drank the tea I had one of these episodes. I remembered vividly the episode with the tea and the steroids. Needless to say, I threw it away when I got home. I sat in that hospital room hoping that my psychic gifts would mystically give me the answer and praying to my angels that they would help the doctors find the answer.

In the end my bloodwork and tests came back normal and after giving me more anxiety meds I was sent home. At this point I was starting to think that maybe I was crazy. I started to wonder what the heck was going on and why it was going on and on. I just didn't understand. I was praying for an answer. Another week went by and although in some ways I felt better I was still very unstable. I still could not eat without being very ill. I felt very toxic. I felt like my body was rejecting anything I put in it. My stomach was acidic, and my system was very weak.

I returned to my original doctor with the same mouth and sinus pressure. Yes, that was still an issue. My teeth were great, and my gums were no longer swollen but I still had the roof of my mouth swelling up. It was getting worse and so were the headaches. At this point they all thought I was crazy. The doctor looked at the roof of my mouth trying to see something and wanting to believe me, but nothing was there. My doctor appeased me anyways and found inflammation and fluid in my nose and ears and put me on an antibiotic. Finally! I knew I had some kind of infection as my cards kept telling me so but no one was treating it! I was so relieved and again thought this was the answer. I took the weekend off of work and decided to go home to Iowa. I was tired of being alone and afraid and thought if I can just be safe and get well I will get through this. I thought I just needed to take the antibiotics and sleep. Another mistake. I had now been given several drugs from various doctors. I found out later that each drug was actually making my issue much worse.

After two days of the antibiotic I found myself on the road driving home. It was a 12-hour drive home to Iowa where my family lived. For the first time in over a week I was hungry again and ate lunch at Perkins, my favorite Midwest place. Although I was tired I made it to my dad's feeling pretty good. I was craving something sweet and stopped at a McDonald's and ordered a chocolate shake. I thought, why not? I had barely eaten in over a month and anything is better than nothing. Again, with the fast food. I reiterate it because it was really such an unhealthy way of living that is totally acceptable in our society. It was making me much more ill than I would have been had I been eating whole foods. So many of us eat the wrong things without even giving it a second thought. I continue to share my choices to show that we really don't think through what we do to ourselves even though at the time it seems okay.

This brings me back to the preface. In the 90 minutes it took me to get to my mom's home from that McDonalds my body had been overcome. Whatever it was that was happening had triggered a massive train wreck that was attacking my entire body. I started with losing my vision in my left eye and seeing only prisms of light. Then it followed with a massive migraine and extreme vomiting. All from a chocolate shake. Yeah that's right.

After falling asleep that night at my mom's; I did wake up. Over the next few days I started to feel better again. I was still unable to eat very much but the headache subsided with some good sleep and my energy slowly began to come back. The anxiety was much of the battle. I had suffered two panic attacks during the previous week and the shakiness and panic continued to come back into my body. I was reluctant to take the anxiety medication I was given…somehow it felt as though I was losing control. Seems ironic now; I was panicking about panicking. Feeling overcome with anxiety and fatigue I was feeling defeated. The night had set in with my new-found depression around the darkness I felt hopeless. My mom wasn't sure what to do for me. She knew I needed to pull out of this, but I really didn't know how to do it. My mom reminded me that, although it was never this severe, I had experienced this kind of anxiety and depression most of my life and that my spiritual work had been what had pulled me out of it. This was very true. Six years prior to this I began my spiritual journey. I had learned to meditate, run energy and ground myself among other things. All of this work led to major life changes including my divorce 3 years prior to this. But my mental health had been much better than it had ever been. Over the last year I sort of put it aside. I was still very much spiritual, but I was not following my meditation practices like I had in the past. I more did it out of convenience or a need for information. Performing readings for my clients was when I was most connected, and it kept me balanced – at least I thought it did.

In taking my mom's advice I drew a bath in her amazingly huge bathtub. I lit some candles and climbed inside. I had so much fear inside of me. I had so much panic that even to quiet my mind and go within created panic. What will I see? What will I hear? Will my mind be crazy? It took a lot of self-control and breathing just to get through the bath. But, at some point in the midst of my breathing through panic and fear I connected.

I saw the angels. I saw Archangel Michael standing in front of me. His presence was so large, and his wings spread the width of the room. I cried. He told me I had to get up. He showed me an image of grabbing my hands and pulling me out of the tub and making me walk. I felt so empowered by this. I felt his strength in every part of my being and so I did exactly what he said. I got up.

I went into the living room and began some basic gentle yoga exercises. My body had been so fatigued I had been lying in bed for weeks. Even the basic postures were challenging but I did them anyway. I woke up the next morning feeling better and each day got better. I was shaky, yes. I still had a difficult time following conversation as my anxiety was so strong. I had somehow created social anxiety and could not lift up my phone, let alone talk to anyone. I only could connect with certain people as other energies were too harsh. I had become incredibly sensitive to everything. After a few more days I began to feel strong again and HUNGRY! I was so excited to feel good for once and to be home with my family that I thought it would be fun for my brother and I to get dinner for my mom and for all of us to watch a movie. We ended up getting pizza from one of our favorite places and rented a comedy. Yes, again with the fast food choices. It was a good night though. The pizza was delicious, and I actually ate more than one piece! I drank a coke for the first time in weeks and didn't get the shakes. We all thought that night that I was finally getting better. Thank Goddess!

But then I woke up the next morning feeling terrible again! Really?! My head, sinuses, ears and mouth were totally swollen. I didn't know what had happened. I felt so good last night and now today again I felt terrible! After an entire day of pain and depression I called my dentist. Could there be something wrong with my mouth? Why is it swollen? Her response was that perhaps it was an allergy. I'd never had any allergies that I knew of. I took the Benadryl per her recommendation anyway and after about an hour the swelling lifted! This was incredible. An allergy? My cards still told me I had an infection, but they were finally saying I was going to have a swift recovery. So, I felt a light at the end of the tunnel. For weeks my cards had shown me that there was no end to my illness. I was hopeful seeing now that there was a resolution in my future.

At this time my cards were also showing me something new. They started to tell me that I had some kind of fungus infection. Fungus? This was odd to me. What even is a fungus infection? I asked my mom and brother about it. Ironically, or shall I say synchronistical, my little brother knew about Candida. He told me that when he had eye problems and went to his optometrist that he told him that he should look into candida. My little brother did some research. He didn't find much information except that it wasn't really recognized by western medicine as an issue and there were only a few specialists in the country that helped people with candida issues. My brother had read of a Doctor in Boulder, CO[19] who did just that and he gave me her information. He had wanted to see her. I can't remember why he hadn't. Maybe because she was out of state or maybe he wasn't ready. I am so grateful he gave me her information. I made an appointment with her, but it would be a couple weeks before I could get in.

Reluctantly, I decided it was time to go home. After months…maybe even more than a year, I was feeling more connected to my spirituality

[19] Dr. Jill Carnahan is an Integrative and Functional Medicine Doctor in Louisville, CO. She is not currently taking new patients but her website is an excellent resource. I highly recommend following her blog and receiving her newsletter. They also can refer doctors in your area. https://www.jillcarnahan.com/

and wanted to connect with my spiritual teachers back home that I trusted to try and help me sort through what was happening. Again, I forced myself to eat some lunch – Wendy's again – and again my mouth swelled. By the time I reached a stopping point on my drive my mouth was in pain and my anxiety running high. I took more Benadryl which relieved the pain and tried to sleep.

Over the next week I was back in the emergency room, had a CT scan and more bloodwork done. Still nothing wrong with my head other than my anxiety. I visited with my teachers in the spiritual community and became armed with information. None of it was about my physical health per se, but I knew better. After all the spiritual work I had done I understood that everything that happens physically is all just energy. It is all just a manifestation of a greater issue within our Selves and our Soul. This gave me momentum and it gave me hope.

Any physical symptoms that occur are a manifestation of emotional baggage.

I began to put things together. This all began in my mouth. What was I doing with my mouth? What was I communicating? What was 'out of alignment' with my mouth and my speech. My spiritual purpose involves communication. What part of my purpose was I not fulfilling? Where had I gone astray? The anxiety and the fear; what was I afraid of? Where was the anxiety coming from? It was all coming from baggage. Baggage I was carrying and baggage I had picked up. Nonsense that I had taken on from other people. It was a heavy load and my body simply could not hold it anymore and it erupted. It started with the eruption of sores in my mouth and spread like wildfire. In addition, these symptoms were teaching me where I had not been properly taking care of myself; my teeth, my food choices and my overall mental state.

I decided to make myself my own client. I began to meditate. I began to take walks again. I had an assignment. I needed to start identifying what were the triggers that causing my emotional and physical reactions. I did an activity each morning when I woke up and each night when

I went to bed. I would center myself through meditation and would review the things that threw me off course. I wrote these triggers down in my journal. I would then work on releasing those energies by placing my palms down on the Earth and asking Mother Earth to help take away what I was carrying. I didn't need it anymore. I remember sitting Creekside at my most favorite meditation spot. A spot I still sit in today. It is on a trail that runs along a creek. It has trees, and, in the past, I have seen beavers here, as well as ducks and deer. I remember sitting at that spot and the sky was grey and I felt so disconnected from myself. I felt weak and tired and like I was floating in depression. I put my hands on the Earth and I felt the dirt and the dead grass that lay there. I looked across the creek and I said out loud; where am I? Please come back I pleaded. Please bring me back. I looked up the metaphysical reason for nausea and insomnia. Nausea is fear and the rejecting of an idea or experience. Insomnia is fear and not trusting the process of life. I started chanting a mantra to heal my anxiety; 'I am safe. I trust the process of life to bring only positive to me.' I asked myself; 'what am I afraid of that my physical symptoms continue to be triggered?' In that process of inner work, I discovered that I was trying to force things to happen in my life; that I was afraid of not being in control. I realized that my physical symptoms were actually an excuse I manifested from my unconscious to hold me back from stepping into my authentic self. By examining my reactions and emotions and repeating positive mantras and practicing releasing the energy I started to feel an energy lift.

I started to get better. I felt energized. I still wasn't sleeping very well and was staying at a friend's house because I couldn't be alone. But I was starting to stand up as the angels had told me to. I forced myself to eat. I started to feel hungry again and crave food. The pain in my head came and went and the Benadryl seemed to treat it. I knew that something was still physically wrong, but I also knew with certainty that my spiritual work was helping me to make progress in my healing. After a week I felt like perhaps I was going to come out of this. I healed a great deal of anxiety through meditation and had completely stopped my panic attacks. Nothing came from all the tests that were done so I was perfectly fine in the medicals' eyes. Still the fatigue went in and out and the pain in my head. After another visit with the channels that I so trusted I decided that this had to stop. Whatever was still going on with me physically needed to end. I drove to the Stupa of Dharmakaya[20]. I go there from time to time to seek refuge and to pray. I had always gone there for things that seem trivial now, like love and money issues. Now I was coming to truly pray. I was truly seeking refuge with the only energies I felt I could trust the most; the Buddha himself.

And so, I went. Tired, out of balance, sick, and with head pains I took the hike up the mountain to the Stupa. I made myself walk. It was cold, and my feet sunk into the snow. But up I went. I listened to the trees and to the wind. I looked at the sky and the Earth. I knew that I was coming home. This was where I was supposed to be. There is a wooden bridge that is beautiful. It crosses over a creek before you make your final ascent to the Stupa. Tibetan prayer flags hang in the trees. Some bright and new and some faded and torn by the wind. I thought to myself; this is where I leave my baggage. I walked across and up to the temple.

In the Stupa I threw myself at the Buddha's feet. I knew that this all had to stop now. I had to end all that I was feeling and all that was happening. I must get well. I must heal. This has gone on way too long. I prayed and prayed and journaled and prayed. Buddha told me not to be afraid....

Journal Entry

Dear Child,

There is nothing to fear. You are carried, by Great teachers and Spirit. Trust. Love – Your Self. Heal thyself. Believe it can be done. Sing. Laugh. Find joy again. Be renewed. Live in your Self, your Spirit. You are to walk a great path. It is time to step on it. Trust that your spirit knows the way. Be Holy. Trust in your intuition. Break free of those who have taken hold and generate fear. Yes, life has changed – but only for the better. Those who have crossed your

---

[20] The Great Stupa of Dharmakaya which liberates upon seeing. https://www. shambhalamountain.org/great-stupa/

path – those lessons are behind you. See what is directly in front of you. You are safe. There is nothing to fear. It is time to follow the teachings you hold so dear. It is time to have clear intentions for your life. No more fragmented thoughts, feelings, reactions, actions and attitudes. Be strong! Be courageous! Command your own power from Spirit! Overcome!

There is nothing holding you back.

There is only what you create.

Become clear. Become focused. Find your strength. Heal thyself.

My health obstacles had become my path to awakening. I knew that the journey to become balanced and whole would also become the platform for my work. Two days later I met with the Functional Medicine doctor and had the beginnings of a diagnosis.

Heal Thyself

Candida. I'd never heard of it before. I spent two days reading multitudes of websites about Candida overgrowth and yeast. I discovered that the beginning of my health problems was actually when I was 3 years old and on antibiotics for chronic tonsillitis and strep. I also discovered that a multitude of candida overgrowth symptoms, much less severe, had been part of my experience all my life. I had a highly acidic stomach; nausea in the morning, fainting and dizzy spells, sugar cravings, a rash under my breasts that seemed as though it was from sweating, athlete's foot, heavy periods, blurry vision, sensitivity to light, headaches, ear infections, canker sores, acne, dark circles under the eyes, insomnia… really, the list goes on and on.

We all have yeast. But because our diet consists mainly of caffeine, sugar, gluten, and yeasty foods we can aid in the growth of the candida or yeast in our bodies. If you add on a weakened immune system and antibiotics or steroids or birth control, hormone shifts etc.…well it becomes a downhill slope to candida land. Between what I was putting in my body and what I was taking trying to fix it I had wrecked my own self. For the first time I was looking in the mirror and truly saw my Self.

***We must be willing to look in the mirror and truly see our Selves.
We must be honest with ourselves about how we are living.***

We truly are what we eat. I had been proud of myself for losing the 50 pounds I had lost. I was feeling better. But I was really just kidding myself. I was ignoring what I was really doing. The endless Starbucks and Diet Coke I was putting into my body. The sugar, not eating regularly, not sleeping, this was all an endless cycle of suffering that truly needed to stop. And it built up inside of my body until my body couldn't take it anymore. All it could do was erupt out of me in a way that would get my attention. Many of us are taking pain pills, antibiotics, caffeine drinks, binging on alcohol…so many things we do to ourselves to ease our suffering. But what are we really suffering from?

It begins in simple human or physical terms. Why do you get constant headaches? Why do you feel better after a couple of beers? Why do you need that hit of caffeine to start your day? These are the mundane questions to begin your journey of self-inquiry. But then it goes deeper. What is so difficult in my life that my body actually feels sick? What in my life is literally making me sick? Am I so angry that I can't see straight? Is my life making me so tired that I literally need to sleep longer? Is my mind so dysfunctional that a beer or a pill is equal to a peaceful meditation? The quick fixes that we have become so dependent on are masking everything inside of us that we need to work on. Our fear of facing ourselves is feeding our need for 'speed' so to speak instead of allowing us to release our suffering. And so, we suffer.

My doctor was fairly certain of what was going on inside of me. She put me on the candida diet immediately along with probiotics. She also set up a large amount of blood work and a fecal test as well. After only 3 days on a diet free of sugar, caffeine, gluten and yeast products my headache was almost completely dissipated. My vision began to clear up and become 'normal' again. My energy began to come back. This process was slow, but I began to feel better and better. Although I was told the cravings would be the worst; they weren't. I was so happy to be feeling so much better that it outweighed everything else. Yes, walking by a coffee shop was difficult and I certainly missed some of my old 'friends'. But I felt better every single day and knew that I was finally on the path to healing. Ironic that a spiritual woman would become ill with something that can only be healed holistically. Heal thyself. Yes, the Teachers were right. It is only our Selves that can truly heal our Selves.

This whole experience is not about a diet. It really isn't about the physical body at all. But our physical body is what teaches us what we need to heal within our Soul. To explain:

We come into the world as a Soul that enters the physical body. We come in with one purpose. To clear the baggage. We come in with karmic baggage from previous lifetimes and we take on new baggage from our parents and family and friends. It's nobody's fault. It's called Samsara. The endless cycle of birth, death and rebirth. It is the great wheel of life that we are constantly spinning in until we become conscious…until we wake up. The Buddhist traditions teach of Samsara and the path of Enlightenment is truly practicing daily to come out of the wheel of suffering and become free. Ultimate liberation. It is my belief at this time in my life that we choose our physical vessels to help us overcome our baggage and to learn and grow within ourselves.

Our body is the vessel to Enlightenment.
Our human experience is The Path.

Each time our body erupts or has symptoms it is the chance to look within ourselves at what is going wrong. It creates an opening for us to discover something about ourselves and to learn. More importantly it is a path to awakening. I read in a book that our obstacles should become our path to healing. And it should be just that. Whether it is a physical symptom, like a cold; or an emotional symptom, such as anger – it is our path to the Truth. If we can overcome our fear of looking within; then we will not only discover the root of our symptom, but we will be able to heal it. In addition, we may be clearing significant pieces of karma from our lifetimes or the lifetimes of the generations in our family.

So now after reading all this you are probably asking; What do I do now? I think the first place to begin is to look at yourself clearly. Look in the mirror. What do you see? This is tricky. If you would have asked me this before the last few months of illness I would have said that I see a beautiful woman who is getting her life together. When in actuality, I was still overweight, unwell, and feeding my food and social addictions on a daily and sometimes hourly basis. There was nothing really in my life that was truly Dharmic or balanced. Everything was hanging on by a thread. Some say they want to live on the edge…but do we really?

These are difficult questions to ask oneself. And the answers can be unpleasant and can even create more obstacles. No one is perfect. Even as I am writing this I am still discovering my own answers. Our life is the journey. Remember that as you begin to heal. Healing becomes your path. This isn't about reaching an end. This isn't about waking up one day and being healthy. This is about going through the process of life and healing your Spirit, so you can move forward in every aspect as a Soul. The first Noble Truth is to recognize that there is suffering.

There is suffering.

Each day that I was sick I was bombarded with images from the television and people in public that there is sickness, disease, afflictions, symptoms, suffering. There is suffering. A woman on television who lost complete control of her mind and spoke gibberish reminds us that we really don't have any control. The hundreds of pharmaceutical commercials selling a drug that can cause nausea, dizziness, swelling, diarrhea, only reminds us that for one symptom we will replace it with another. The older woman in a wheelchair because she is unable to move. The man who has to carry with him air to breath because his lungs are no longer strong. There is suffering. The suffering of others is what empowered the Buddha to leave his life of luxury and go off into the world. He wanted to end suffering. Aren't we all just like Siddartha[21]? Don't we all want to end suffering?

I committed long ago that I would give myself over to spirit to help others. I have re-committed and been re-initiated onto the path by many spiritual teachers, healers...even His Holiness the Dalai Lama himself! I never hesitate to commit to my path to heal others. Yet, I did resist on the physical level. My greatest initiation, my greatest teacher has been yeast. She has taught me so much in such a short amount of time about where I have been imbalanced and where I have not been serving my higher self. And it has come far from food. I truly feel I am a good person. I care about all of you I've met and haven't met. I want to heal and help and be strong. Ah...but there is still an ego. After my divorce I longed to be free. To date, to experience life. To live differently. My spiritual self was put on hold while my lust, desire and anger took over. I wanted to look good and feel good...but in such a superficial way. Deep down I think I knew what I was striving for really but on the outside my friends, my social hours and my looks were what were important. I'm not saying I was running around completely careless and callous – my friends who know me know me better than that – but what I wasn't giving any thought to and what I wasn't caring about was my own Self. For Pete's sake! I wasn't actually honoring the most important thing in my life. Me!

In the end our suffering comes from something very simple. Baggage.
Our baggage creates belief systems that cause us to think less of ourselves.
From a low self-worth comes the belief that we
are no longer perfect and of the divine.
Because we are no longer perfect we begin to suffer.
In suffering we begin to medicate ourselves, creating more suffering.
The deeper suffering creates deeper symptoms,
creating even more suffering.
The suffering leads to more medications, creating even more suffering.

---

[21] Siddartha Gautama lived in Nepal during the 6th to 4th century. He would become known as the Buddha.

And this continues to cycle…and can lead to suicide,
cancer, emotional issues, crises, and so on.
This is Samsara.

The only way to heal this cycle is to come out of it. The only way to come out of it is to become conscious. The only way to become conscious is to begin to practice awareness. The best way to do this is through the spiritual practices. Through meditation, journaling, exercise, chanting, and working with incredible healers and doctors that you trust.

My disclaimer here is that this isn't about stopping all your medications or even giving up caffeine. This process must be subtle. And you must partner with specialists. You must find a doctor you can trust that can truly help you with your medical conditions. You must find healers and teachers that you also trust that can guide you through the processes. You must find what connects to you. Buddhism may not be what you connect with. It may be another form of religion or no religion at all. This is your path. There will be no simple answer and there is no answer that fits all.

What I do believe that 'fits all' is what I am sharing with you here. I believe that we MUST understand our suffering. We MUST become consciously aware of our own selves and begin the basic practices of healing. I believe the following process contains the four steps necessary to create an awakening that leads to profound healing:

Become aware – Come out of Samsara. Be willing to complete self-inquiry exercises. Practice mindfulness.

Become wise – Find the teachers, doctors and healers that you trust that can help you to begin your journey. Find out as much information as you can about your body and yourself. Learn all you can. Study different spiritual practices and find what works for you. Take different exercise courses to find what works for you. Read and Study.

Practice - You must practice all that you are learning. Meditating and practicing mindfulness daily. The more you practice the more solid you become in your Self and your Spirit. The practice is The Path and The Way.

TRUST – Faith is the most important piece. You have to trust in yourself and in the Divine. You have to trust that you are always safe in the hands of Spirit. When you do not trust you must go back to the beginning with self-inquiry. What is it that I do not trust?

This is the path. It is only my opinion – my process. It has worked for me time and time again and I do believe it will work for you as well. It will work for anyone at any age. This is how you begin to heal yourself. This is not about a quick fix or a do it yourself kit. The best part about healing yourself is you are not alone; AND, you don't have to do it alone. This is about partnership and connection with those you trust the most. But, you and you alone must do the work.

> *We are all one energy, interconnected, woven together.*
> *But in this world, we also have separate vessels. We*
> *must do the work alone and on our own. Yet, in doing*
> *our 'own' work, we are actually healing all others.*
> *Heal thyself.*
> *Heal your family.*
> *Heal your friends.*
> *Heal thy enemies.*
> *Heal the world.*

Journal Entry

What am I using to medicate myself? Tylenol, Caffeine, Television, Anti-depressants etc.

Where am I self-medicating? Constantly on the phone or out socially, alcohol etc.

Is my body physically healthy? Proper weight, proper diet, illness etc.

Am I happy?

BECOME AWARE

PURIFY. ENERGIZE. HEAL

2

Sacred Space, Meditation and Contemplation

Your Spiritual Foundation

"Promises, like pie crust, are made to be broken. But a pie crust that is able to hold in even the most difficult of fillings has the strength equal to that of a promise made to heal the Self." Lisa Toal

When you begin to make a crust you first cut sticks of butter into flour. You can do this with a fork, with a pastry cutter, or your fingers. The goal is to create small pea sized balls of flour and butter. You then add milk or water until it becomes a dough. You are taking three forms; liquid, fat and wheat, and making it into one form that is stronger and able to withstand the baking process while holding in a filling. It is important not to overwork the dough or it will become stiff and will not be the flaky crust you want; but instead become hard and chewy. Although there are only 3 ingredients in a pie crust, it can be very easy to ruin it; by adding too much of one ingredient or by mixing too much or too little.

This process is much like beginning the work to bring your life into balance. You begin with the ingredients or the building blocks of living. This is step one. Become aware. This is your foundation, your crust. If you overwork yourself in this process your energy will become static and the work will become hard. Giving just the right amount of time and energy into your foundation will bring about the desired result.

To achieve perfect health; you must be balanced.
To be balanced; you must build a foundation
of practice that develops awareness.
As you begin those practices; you must still create balance.
Everything in moderation.

The tools given here are providing you with behaviors that you will carry for a lifetime. They are the tools that you will go back to again and again. In the hardest of times it is the simplest of practices that can have the most profound effect. By mixing these tools together, you are creating a foundation to 'hold' all the pieces or 'filling' in your life together.

Just like there are ingredients in a pie crust; there are tools that provide the foundation for healing. A tool belt to create awareness. This is the natural place to begin as the journey to awareness unfolds through this process. Whatever you are going through in your life whether it be physical, spiritual, mental or emotional; these behaviors are what will act as a guide to release you from your suffering. Once you learn and understand how to put these practices into place you will find that they can move you through a crisis with ease and will provide some comfort in times that are uncomfortable.

Where do I begin my practice?

Sacred Space

"This is my simple religion. There is no need for temples, no need for complicated philosophies. Our brain, our own heart is our temple; the philosophy is kindness." HH Dalai Lama

What is Sacred Space? I began to write this section detailing the nuts and bolts of sacred space. Then one day, a few weeks ago, I went for my daily run on my usual trail by the creek. I usually run three miles out and walk the three miles back. At the three-mile point there is a dirt path that connects to the sidewalk. It leads down a small hill to a sandy bank on the side of the creek. I love this space. I sit and meditate and have, at times, even done yoga creek side. There are many tall trees. The creek is wide in this particular location and breaks in the middle where a tall tree has grown right out of the water. Last spring there was a Beaver damn here and I even had the blessing of seeing the Beavers before they tore it down and moved on. On this particular day it felt much like fall. The sun was shining, and it was warm. However, the air was crisp and smelled of burnt wood. The leaves on the trees had changed to golds and even browns and some of them were even scattered on the ground. I sat down next to my favorite tree with my feet dangling above the water. There was a slight breeze. You could hear the rustling of the leaves and the water flowing and bubbling around itself and the big tree in the center of the creek. At that moment I thought to myself how wonderful this space was. How blessed I was to be sitting there at that moment. It was not long before that I sat here feeling completely out of sorts. Now here I was running and healthy and my body had found peace. I took in the scene with a deep breath and instead of closing my eyes to meditate I just watched. I watched a golden leaf spiral in the currents of the water as it floated past me. I watched the birds fly back and forth between the almost barren trees. I saw the sunlight shown through the trees and sparkle on the water's edge. I listened also. I listened to the sound of the wind. It told me that winter was coming, and this moment would soon be gone. The energy of that moment and that space felt like home to me. It felt warm and soft and comforting. This space had become very dear to me over the year that I have lived there, and many tears, joys and healings had taken place there. That is when it hit me.

This is Sacred Space! It is not an altar that you create or barrier in your home just for meditating. It is a special place. A place where you feel at home. A place where you can take your troubles and your joys and 'hold' them there until you are ready to release them. It can be likened to a mothers' womb where everything is sacred and life-giving…a creative force that no one can name or point out but instead you must sense it.

It is filled with the energy of the heart. Opening the center of all seven centers filling you with healing, compassion and light.

Sacred Space does not need to be created as you already carry it.

It may reveal itself in nature, in a statue of a Goddess, in a favorite chair or in a scent you cannot forget. Sacred Space is that place where you feel one with God and ultimately connected to yourself.

Why must one have Sacred Space? What is the point and purpose of it? Sacred space is where you do your 'work'. It is the space where you can meditate, journal, throw a card or even just contemplate. It is a space that you journey to when you need to think, when you need to cry, or when you need to light a candle for a friend in need. By returning to the same space time and time again you create a vibration, or an energy. This is an energy of healing and of light; of intuitiveness and of creativity. Just like a writer may have a writing room or a painter a studio; you too must have a sacred space. And you can have more than one. You can have a favorite garden outside and a favorite chair inside. You can go all out and have an altar with candles and deities and cards and incense, or simply light a candle in your bedroom. The beauty of your sacred space is that it is just that; your own. My only advice is to 'feel' out what space is best for you and to go back to it each time you are working on yourself. This will create an energy, a vibration of healing that will bring you back to yourself each time you enter it.

Meditation

"Why are we so petrified of silence? Here, can you handle this?...Did you think about your bills, your ex, your deadlines; or when you think you're gonna die. Or did you long for the next distraction?" Alanis Morrisette

Meditation is the foundation of all healing work. ALL healing work. If you are learning to develop your gifts, completing inner work, wanting peace in your life, or just want to connect with Spirit; this is where it all begins. It is my opinion that meditation should not only be the first thing taught but should be reviewed again and again as it is where we connect to our Truth. I am not certain that meditation can ever be perfected in a lifetime and it is also not my belief that should be the goal. My philosophy on meditation is that practice makes perfect and perfect is the idea of connecting, becoming neutral and listening. Any ideas that the mind will be totally clear after a few deep breaths is almost unattainable to me. To me, meditation is not about clearing the mind but instead, watching the mind. For those of you that are sensitive; as soon as you clear your mind then the Spirit world begins to speak, filling you with all sorts of new pictures and ideas than the shopping list your mind was first reviewing.

Coming to a totally present state where your mind is clear is the goal...it is in that place that clarity of purpose and next steps will finally come into place.

Are you staring into a blank space? No, of course not. You are just listening and becoming aware of what is there deep inside you vs. the chatter from the outside world.

Meditation begins with breathing. The first thing most people think of when they think of meditation is a picture of a person sitting in lotus position with their eyes closed and their mind clear. There is no need for this. Sit in a comfortable chair, lie on the floor...the only thing I don't recommend is lying in bed. You are sure to fall asleep! Now, if you do fall asleep when trying to meditate; give yourself permission! You are obviously tired. I once had a student that fell asleep every time she meditated for the first 3 months! She finally caught up on the rest her body needed from years of working long hours and was able to hold a concentrated meditation. Whatever you do, as you go through the process; do NOT beat yourself up for doing something 'wrong'. The beauty of this work is that nothing is 'wrong'. Everything happens exactly as it should. Being aware that what you are experiencing is the key to the whole process.

Back to breathing.
This is where you start.

Once you are comfortably situated begin to breathe. Just begin by breathing normally. Notice your belly. When you breathe in, your belly should fill with air. When you breathe out, it should go in. Most Americans breathe incorrectly. You may find right away that you are not filling up the lungs and diaphragm area properly. A great technique is to lay flat on a flat surface; such as the floor or even a table. Breathe in and out. Feel your stomach. Where is the air going? How does it feel? How deep does the breath go? Ideally you want to fill up the diaphragm in the lower abdomen first, then the lungs, and then as your release; you release the lungs first, then the diaphragm. It takes practice just to breathe. You would be surprised at how much work that can take. The diaphragm is a muscle just like any other and you will need to 'work it out' for a while before you feel you can take deep breaths. I read a statistic once that we only have about 40% fresh air in our lungs at a time. If you can get yourself to a point where you breathe in for 8 counts, out for 8 counts, 8 times in a row; you will then 100% fresh air in your lungs. You may also be dizzy, but it is great for cleaning out the body.

The best way to breath is 'in and out' breathing. It is the process of breathing in through the nose and out through the mouth. The purpose of this is that the nose provides a natural filter so the air you are bringing in is more concentrated and is cleaner. When you release from the mouth you are truly releasing and relaxing the body. Spend some quality time with your breath. Notice how your lungs and diaphragm feel and notice how clear your mind is when you are thinking so hard about breathing and nothing else!

Once you have the breathing down, the next piece of meditation is clearing the mind, so you can come into a neutral space. There are some great visualizations to aid with this. You first start with your breathing. Just getting into a rhythm can take a few minutes and this will begin the process of clearing the mind and body. The next practice you can add to this is 'mindfulness'. This is the art of becoming 'mindful' of the body. It is really awareness. Notice your body. Have you ever had a bruise just show up and you don't remember how it got there? Being aware of your physical body can be a real eye opener. Notice where you hurt or have aches. Notice where you feel good. Notice how you are sitting or lying down. Just notice. You can also do this with your emotional and energy bodies. How do you feel? How does your energy feel? You do not need to know anything about energy to do this exercise. You inherently 'know' what is energetically blocked or stuck in your field. Just ask yourself and it will come to you. Mindfulness and breathing are two great ways to get started with your meditation. It will automatically clear a lot of thoughts that were running through your mind before you sat down.

The next thing that you can do is begin to notice your thoughts. You might be thinking, I hope I can get my mind clear while I try this meditation thing? Or, I hope my dog doesn't start barking while I am trying to be quiet. Recognize the thought and watch it as though it did not belong to you. My favorite visualization is to imagine the thought in a balloon. Then float it away. This sends the energy and the thought away bringing your mind back to the present. You can also flush these thoughts down the toilet or any other technique you wish to use. The idea is to clear it from your mind, so you come back to the present moment.

This is really the basics of meditation. You will find as you have things to contemplate or begin working on developing your sensitive gifts that the basics become simple and you can spend hours 'inside' just working with energies. One of the best behaviors I learned from a teacher is to 'take in' to your meditation things you want to accomplish. This could be working through an energy, a healing you would like to do on someone, or some inner work you want to do on yourself. This gives you some real things to do while you are sitting with your eyes closed… you'd be surprised at how quickly time will pass! In the beginning, don't worry about how long or short you are 'in'. Just focus on practicing the simple techniques and don't give up.

Contemplation

"What we plant in the soil of contemplation, we shall reap in the harvest of action." Meister Eckhart

Whenever I hear this word I think of the Monty Python skit where philosophers are playing soccer. As soon as the whistle blows; instead of playing they all put their hands to their chin and begin contemplating. Finally, one of them gets an idea and kicks the ball and scores. It is hilarious if you have that sense of humor! This is precisely describing the idea behind contemplation. Rather than 'reacting' to a situation in your life you think about it. You take the time to 'hold' it in your space for a while. This not only prevents you from doing something stupid but can also provide you with an answer or a solution totally different than what you expected. It is really a process of slowing down and taking stock rather than acting rashly or from an emotional space.

It is easy to contemplate but not easy to remember to contemplate.

Many times, we do something out of fear, worry or stress; rather than out of a peaceful state of the heart. How many times have you gone to bed and awoke in the morning realizing that you would have done something totally different than you did the night before?

The best way I can describe contemplation is by going back to the pie analogy. If you make a pie and serve it before it's cooked…it is just not going to be good. You put it in the oven. It bakes. The oven 'holds' it for an hour or so. It keeps it in a safe space where it takes everything that you put together and solidifies it. When you take it out, it has been fully cooked. You then set the pie on a rack and let it cool. Again, another resting period. Finally, it is time to cut into it and serve it. This is precisely the act of contemplation. You begin with an idea or a situation; a question or an issue that needs resolution. You take it and 'hold' it. Just like the oven. You will hold that issue in your consciousness for an hour, a day or even a week or month depending on what it is. There is no need to think about it all the time or even to write about it all the time. Just by choosing to 'hold' it, you are doing just that. You may have dreams about it. You may journal about it. You may wake up one morning and know the answer. The idea behind it is that when it is 'cooked' you will become totally clear on what to do. Once you know what to do there is again a 'cooling' or resting period. You write down what it is that you are to do and leave it yet again. You allow it to manifest in the right time with right action. Then you act on the information you received. Now, this sounds wonderful but is not as easy as it looks.

Let's say you have a fight with a friend. Our natural reaction is to try and fix it right away. Can you imagine waiting and instead contemplating your next step? Once you know what that is can you imagine waiting just a bit longer before acting on it? I guarantee you will not react the way you would have in the moment, you will not solve it the way you originally intended and by waiting you also eliminated much of the 'drama' that may have occurred had you continued to push the situation. It is a great lesson for those of us who are impatient…and there are many of us that are.

What I love about contemplation is you can apply it to anything in your life and you will always get your answer.

Journal Entry

Where or What is my Sacred Space?

Complete the following activities over a 2-week time period:

Activity 1. Build your sacred space.

Activity 2. Practice Meditation and Belly Breathing.

Activity 3. Contemplative practice: Up to this point you have journaled about your current state of health and overall happiness. What conclusions do you draw from those journaling exercises? How do you think you have already changed?

3

The Practice of Journaling
and Self-Inquiry

Journaling

Do you keep a diary? Do you write in a journal? Many of us have two or three journals we have either bought or been given lying around our house. A percentage of those that do have written in the first two or three pages and the rest is left blank. Within all of us, there are a choice few who write in one every day and are diligent in their practice. Journaling can feel like a chore. Some days you may not want to do it and other days you may want to write for hours. You may write in a journal to answer the questions that come up in this book, you may write the morning pages from The Artist's Way. The point is to write. To sit down each day and write. I agree that the morning is the best time to write. You will experience more of a stream of consciousness when you first wake up then when you go to bed at night. I admit that I write most often. I do write when I wake up but continue to throughout the day as things come to me. I also do love to write late at night when the spirits are most active. In the end, what you want to do with your journaling is really up to you. I have one student who has a different journal for each thing she writes; one for homework, one for dreams, one for books she is reading and so on. I have another student who has the most beautiful journals and she writes fluidly in them until they are full. Then there is me; who has notepads on her desk, journals in her bed, computers on her lap, and a small notebook in my kitchen. Whatever works. Again, just write. You can write about your day, you can write your shopping list, you can complete inner work, you can write a story. Writing is the key. It provides a deep connection within yourself. Writing can also move energy. If you are sad and you write it all down, it will clear it from your mind and energy field. If you are mad, writing it out can diffuse the anger and even provide a solution to your problem.

**Journaling is the single most important
tool to 'cleaning out your soul'.
Enough said.**

I know these are only brief descriptions of these tools, but this will certainly get you started. You will find that having a sacred space and practicing; daily meditation, mindfulness, contemplation and journaling will always bring you back to your Self.

**These practices will provide you with a space that
is just for you in the midst of the chaos of the world.
In this space you will create awareness.**

Self-Inquiry

The process of self-inquiry is the most challenging of all the awareness practices. It is certainly the most uncomfortable. Learning to meditate, although challenging for some, brings peace and tranquility in the midst of our daily lives. To contemplate and journal brings answers we were not expecting and clarity to our opportunities in the world. Self-inquiry; the act of asking yourself the questions necessary to work through your blocks; this can create tension, frustration, anger and static. However, once you are able to overcome the 'destructive emotions' that arise with self-inquiry; you will find release, acceptance and forgiveness.

*O Great Buddha! I don't know where to
begin. Have I been unconscious?
Have I sat deep within the forest unable to see thru the trees?
Yes. And a great many lessons I have learned.*

Containment. Patience. Discernment.
In our exhausting effort to prove self-worth; we give too much away.
In our unending quest to live the vision of our life
tomorrow; we fail to live in the challenge of today.
We struggle.
We are afraid.
Is it not the fear deeply rooted in the dark
spaces of our hearts what drives us?
And I wonder; where does it lead?
We must live our mistakes.
We must experience loss.
We must lie naked, in the dark, alone and afraid.
Seek Guidance.
Seek shelter in the bosom of the present moment.
Taste Life.
Touch Thought.
Live in the fullness that if no one hears your whispers
of wisdom that so too; it reaches all ears.
And so we live as we die.
In pain and in silence; fear and grace.
Touched by God.
Held by the angels.
Dancing in dreams of afterlife.

When I am ready to 'face' myself and ask the difficult questions necessary to bring balance and healing to my Soul; where do I begin?

What a question! Where do any of us begin? We are all unique. We have different problems, different challenges and different beliefs. One might struggle in one compartment of their life and someone another. In my own process I have developed a system that has worked for me. I am hopeful that this systematic approach will be easy to apply for anyone who wants to begin asking the difficult questions in their life. I began by creating compartments for my life. As each one carries its own importance; I believe each compartment carries equal weight.

Compartments look like: Romance, Relationships, Career, Spirituality, Health and so on.

Complete the following activity and self-inquiry exercises over a 2-week time period:

Activity 1. Create a Pie Chart for your life. Draw a circle on a piece of paper. Create a 'pie' chart of your life.

Journal Entry

What are the compartments that make up your life?

How much time are you spending on each one?

Are you creating a balance between these compartments?

So many of us work too much. Our pie chart becomes imbalanced almost immediately when we look at how much we are at the office or in our place of employment. There are others who spend too much time attending social gatherings and events and no time alone. And I cannot forget those that spend all of their time taking care of everyone else and never do anything for themselves. Whether you are a worker or a giver or a social butterfly; there is imbalance. I want to say here; Please, take your time completing this pie chart of your life. Do not rush through it. Contemplate your compartments. Meditate on your life and look at it as though you were watching a movie. Take in how you have been living and the choices you have made. Do NOT go a step further until you have truly looked at the different aspects of your life from an honest perspective. If you do not complete this first step honestly and methodically, your work following this will be only touching the surface and will not serve you in reaching your Truth.

Once you have completed your pie chart you have discovered exactly where to begin.

This is only the beginning. A place to start. It reads on the packaging of medications prescribed by doctors; the doctor has made the decision that the risks involved in prescribing the medication outweigh the benefits to the patient. This is very true with self-inquiry. Side effects of self-inquiry are: anger, frustration, sadness, moodiness, weepiness, confusion, fear, desire, shame, guilt, blame. The healing results are: happiness, joy, understanding, acceptance, forgiveness, grace, Light, Truth, harmony, balance, patience, gratitude and peace.

The practices of meditation, contemplation, journaling and self-inquiry begin the process to 'become aware'. Once awareness of the mind begins to unfold; there is greater awareness. The awareness of All Things.

Complete the following self-inquiry exercises upon completion of this chapter. You can take as long as you'd like to complete these. The goal is to complete these questions before moving on to the next chapter.

Journal Entry

Where in my life have I become imbalanced?

Just take that question in.

Contemplate.

Journal.

Meditate.

What have I discovered about myself?

How does this make me feel?

What is this teaching me?

How have I learned from this?

What am I not honoring within myself that has created this imbalance?

What emotions come 'up' for me when I complete this exercise?

What are these emotions teaching me?

What do I learn from these emotions?

What is my level of awareness currently? Around my health? Around my overall happiness?

4

Mindfulness of the Body

It is only fitting that part of our weight loss journey partners with mindfulness of the physical body. In the world we know today our physical bodies take a beating. We work tireless hours and are often running from place to place. We do not give ourselves time to eat or exercise properly. We find ourselves tired, overworked and often with little to no energy to maintain even the simplest health routine. In addition, we do not pay much attention to our bodies. We are not aware of what is happening to them in the present moment; our minds are always focused elsewhere.

How many times have you found a bruise or cut on your body and you do not even remember how it got there? Has your body become stiff or sore and yet you are unsure of what might have caused it? Do you sometimes feel bloated or nauseous and thought perhaps you just weren't feeling well? Do you take aspirin for a headache without wondering why the headache was there in the first place?

Getting connected with your body is truly the first step in discovering the cause of your weight gain. If you do not know what your body needs or feels; how then can you support it?

Activity 1. The Mindfulness of the Body Practice

Sit in a chair or on a meditation cushion. Ensure your space is quiet and you will not be disturbed. Begin breathing in through your nose and out through your mouth. With each breath, breathe more deeply, taking in more and more fresh air and releasing the stale air in your lungs.

Notice Your Body and complete the following self-inquiry questions.

Journal Entry

How does my body feel?

Where do I feel pain? Soreness? Inflexible? Heavy?

Where do I feel light? Open? Strong?

Now begin to place your hands on your body. Put your hands on the areas of your body where you carry weight.

Ask yourself the following self-inquiry questions.

How does this weight feel?

What emotion is here?

What other messages/images/thoughts/feelings come up for me when I touch this area? For example; you may place your hands on your stomach and see a yellow light or feel the anxiety of your life being carried in this space. By becoming aware of what is going on within your own physical body, you will begin to build a relationship with it. You will begin to understand what is causing the excess weight and also what emotional issues you may need to work on. Spend at least 20-45 minutes a day with this exercise for at least 7 days. Journal what comes to you as messages/thoughts/feelings daily.

5

Mindfulness of the Emotional Body

In this chapter we are going to focus on our emotional body. What is the emotional body? This is a subtle energy field that surrounds your physical body. It is also directly connected to our energy centers or chakras, as well as the other energetic bodies in our field such as our aura and our energy channels. The emotional body carries the emotion and/or baggage that we have carried in this lifetime and potentially other lifetimes as well. There is an excellent practice to examine the emotional body.

Activity 1. Sit in a chair or on a meditation cushion. Ensure you are in a quiet space without distraction. Take a few minutes to breathe deeply, eyes closed, and place yourself in a meditative state. Once you have quieted your mind; imagine that you are made of glass. Visualize your body as though it were crystal. The idea here is that you are able to see through yourself as though it were a clear glass. Once you have that image in your mind; imagine that you are able to see your emotions on and in this crystal image. A couple of examples could be that there is a great deal of red paint on your heart, indicating that you have anger in your heart center. You could also see cracks in your glass around your throat, indicating that you have had communication issues. These are just a couple examples of the thousands of visualizations you can have on your body of glass. Take time to look at your body of glass and to take note of what you see. You may not understand what it all means at first but as information unfolds you will discover more about your emotional body and where your emotions may be sitting in your physical body.

Once you have worked with this visualization; you can begin to go deeper into the images that you are uncovering. Perhaps you want to know where the communication issues first came from? Or maybe you want to understand more about the anger in your heart center. Take time each day with your journal before and after meditation to write any thoughts/feelings that come up through this process.

Our emotions are a trigger when it comes to when and what we eat. Most of us have diets that are stress based. When we are stressed, frustrated, hormonal etc.; we find ourselves eating sugary foods or drinking alcohol. This portion of self-inquiry and meditation is about tracking how you are emotionally eating and also getting to the deeper issue; which is why these emotions come up in the first place.

Your homework for this chapter is to meditate on your body of glass and to begin to understand the emotions that you carry in your physical body. You also will begin to track in your food journal when you are eating due to an emotional trigger.

Complete the following Self-inquiry questions over a minimum of a 7-day period. You can continue to go back to this meditation and self-inquiry practice at any time as more comes up for you.

Journal Entry

Reflect on the Body of Glass Meditation

Journal Entry

What emotions were I experiencing over this week that caused me to eat?

What did I choose to eat due to this emotion?

What part of my body 'lights up' when I am eating this food?

What emotion do I feel once I ate the food?

Where does this emotion come from?

How is this emotion serving me right now?

How was this process for you?

How did it feel to have to focus on your emotions? When we start to look at our emotional triggers, it can be a great awareness but at the same time it can also bring up a great deal of frustration. We find ourselves feeling guilt or shame about what we do to ourselves.

Journal Entry

Why can't I stop myself from eating?

Why am I unable to stop myself from eating foods I know are not good for me?

Why am I so angry?

Where is this sadness coming from?

Our emotions directly affect our diet.

Now that you understand how your emotions are affecting your diet and your choice of foods; now it is time to look deeper at those emotions and how to release them. Complete the next exercise and self-inquiry questions over a 7-day time period.

Activity 2. Physical Exercise

Physical exercise is a great way to release emotion. When we are angry, frustrated, sad, stressed, overwhelmed etc.; finding ourselves at the gym is a much better outlet than in the candy aisle at the local grocery store. There are hundreds of great physical activities that can help release emotion: running, yoga, weights, walking. As you move now in this journal; it is time to begin to bring an exercise routine into your life in addition to continued changes in your diet based off your food journal. Take a yoga class, go for a walk each day, run every night. Choose an activity that is healthy for you and that works in partnership with your physical body. Regardless of what shape you are currently in; any kind of active movement each day this next week is going to help.

The second piece of this assignment is connected with your emotional body work. Take the top 3 emotions that continued to come up for you. Choose one of those emotions to 'take in' to your exercise routine. While you are actively moving; think about that emotion.

Journal Entry

How did that emotion affect me over the course of this last week?

How does my body feel while I think of this emotion?

Where is this emotion in my body?

As you are thinking of these questions you are literally 'working out' your emotions through physical movement. After contemplating this emotion during the course of your exercise routine you will then imagine it releasing. See the energy of that emotion as a color or a symbol and imagine it changing into a bright light and dissolving.

Exercise at least 3 times this week. Each time focus on a different emotion that was significant for you.

Continue your journal.

Continue your mindfulness of the body practice daily.

6

Healing Your Ancestry

As I mentioned before; part of my process of trying to heal was to seek wisdom from other channels and healers that I had come to trust in the metaphysical community. I gathered all of the messages from these gifted healers and started working on the homework they had given me. Some of the most intense information I received was about my family and my lineage. I was told that as a little child or even before you come into the world you make an agreement to accomplish specific lessons. Some of those lessons you want to learn come through the lineage you decide to incarnate through. These lessons are lessons of change. Physical symptoms are only recognition that you need to get back on track. I was told that I needed to research my family history and come to a better understanding of what I had inherited and what I was to learn. I was also told by another healer and channel that Candida was actually a symptom of fear. That the candida was a result of the fear that women in my family many generations ago had because of their psychic gifts. They had to hide their gifts, and some were afraid for their lives. This fear and panic manifested into a larger physical issue that passed down through the generations.

Well how does that work you might wonder? I wasn't sure and began the process of doing the activities I was given to work on my family lineage. I wrote the full names of the women in my family starting with myself and then going back 7 generations. I placed it on my altar and began to meditate. I didn't see pictures per se but what I did feel was a lot of stress. I felt anger and sadness and fear. I knew that these women had not had it easy and somehow, I was taking on a lot of that energy through the illness I was experiencing in the physical body. We do take on energy from all kinds of sources and we can take it on from our lineage as much as we can take it on from a past life.

I spent a lot of time talking to my mom about the family history and what she knew about my grandmother, great grandmother and beyond. These women were pioneer women, farm women and they had tough lives. A couple had marriages to abusive men and a couple had health issues. My mom also struggled with health issues all through her childhood. In talking to my mom and trying to understand my family history I realized I had so much in common with these women; my struggle with my health was just one of them. There were many similarities with these women in my own experiences with relationships as well. My great grandmother was one of these women and an incredible spirit. I admire her ability to stay positive even when her life was not always easy. She trusted in the way of things. She wrote this letter to my grandmother many years ago. It shares a lot about how her life was. It's beautifully written and explains her struggle and her thoughts on how to stay present.

Now that you know more about life and its demands, you have a clearer view of the struggle for existence of me and my children. Much of it was my fault. I was an ignorant little country girl anxious to better my situation and it was a way out to marry your dad and learn about a different life away from the drudgery that I was forced into to look after Jay and Dad's farm interests. I even took enough of the milk money and went by train to Chatek and wanted to live with my Mother and Dad hoping to finish High School and have a good chance for a suitable life for my early teen years. NO pa said. I want you to stay on the farm and look after Jay. That is when your dad came on the scene. Dad took me to the depot in Chatek and bought my ticket; no change in my pocket. There on the train was your dad going down to Garden Valley to work for Jan on Dad's farm. He was very well dressed and had an attitude of the world I didn't know about. He had me sit beside him in his seat. He had some fine luggage he moved over for a place for me and my little old suitcase. I began to feel at ease and important. Jay met the train in Humbard and was all smiles when he knew that Norm was coming to work on the farm which was his intention. Norm was really fun. He was neat and clean, had a great sense of humor. He was quite a good cook. He had learned to cook while on a job in the logging woods as a cook's helper. I didn't know then all there was about cooking. So he helped me some in the kitchen too. He could bake cake, cook meat and make pancakes etc. Jay was running after Liona and her family and was glad to leave responsibility for me at home with Norm for company and help. I soon found your dad had itchy feet and was thinking of leaving. I was tired of washing clothes on a washboard, cleaning, washing huge milk cans every day, dressing chickens, gathering eggs and packing them in crates. Jay took them to town and exchanged the eggs for groceries. A nice lady, a friend of my mothers, told me she saw Jay in the store buying groceries with our egg money for Liona's folks. But he bought only part of my list. Liona's dad wasn't much account. He used to come over with his team and wagon and load up grain and feed for his two cows and the horses and his dog was all he had. I didn't know it when Liona got pregnant. Soon a wedding was arranged. I now had to make Liona a dress for the wedding, arrange for the reception – everything. Your dad had asked me to marry him some time before that. We went with Jay and Liona to Humberd to the justice of the peace to get married. Nobody got any papers to show marriage. He was a stupid old man. However later he sent Jay and Liona a sort of certificate but we never got one. I think your dad knew better so much later we went by train over into Minnesota to one of those quick marriage places and were married by a judge. Got a wedding certificate which by the way was lost on that wild trip to Arizona. Or maybe when we went to North Dakota and worked for Bradford Ranch at AYR, North Dakota. (now framed on the wall at Aunt B's) I had so much to learn. I knew very little about a world outside of my birth home at Garden Valley and the little town of Humberd where I spent two years of high school. I had a bad place to stay, had to go home weekends, 6 miles from home (this was all before ma and pa moved to Chatek) Jay or Pearl drove a team to Humberd to bring me home weekends. That soon wasn't satisfactory, and I was removed from high school in my sophomore year. Then mother and dad bought the home in Chatek and moved up there and I was left on the farm with Jay. That was when life became empty for me. This friend of mothers, fanny Dunn, told my mother they should take me to Chatek and given me a chance to grow up and learn a better life then just staying and working for Jay on the farm. But of course, she didn't. Bitter disappointment. With responsibility your dad lost his charm and any ideas of a substantial home life. He really never grew up. Wanted to stay young and go places and do impossible things or nothing at all. As you will remember that ended after we finally reached Seattle.

Meeting and marrying Glenn wasn't perfection. (only grandfather my own mother knew) but I was never hungry after that. And I was always assured of shelter and kind treatment for me and my family. Glenn was far from perfect. He never wanted to be. He was ready to have a life of his own making and you know all of it from there. From his ability and my help and ability I can now live comfortably where I am. I am told that your dad never really grew up. Treated his second family much the same as he did with us and died penniless. I don't want to dwell in a hopeless past. I read a timely article in Reader's Digest. It said remember the past if you wish but don't dwell on it. The past is gone forever tomorrow hasn't come yet today is here now live it! Good advice. These curiosities and conclusions brings up memories that has explanations in my mind and heart. Heartaches better forgotten. Some of us have to learn the hard way. I am happy where I am, and I intend to keep it that way. A lifetime struggle is ending well and I am at peace with progress I have made. This letter may not make much sense, but it covers a lifetime of various experiences. Norman was not gifted with feelings of responsibility. I expect he couldn't change his natural characteristics. He wanted to be a free spirit and yet have what he wanted. If this is not a good valentine letter but I have confided deep secrets that is my business and struggle and you are the only one I have confided with. Good breakfast, hot cereal, toast grapefruit etc. Going to have raviola for dinner.

I remember I was very young. I'm not sure of the age but I had to have been only 6 or 7. I remember her farm. There were very tall trees, and everything was a very deep green. There was no sign of death or foliage that was not taken care of. Everything was thriving and almost overgrown in appearance. I remember walking with her to feed the cows. I must have done this more than once as I remember being excited to go. I was afraid to feed the large green kale leaf to the dairy cow. It seemed so big and dangerous. I'm sure the cow thought this was funny considering it was such a docile animal. She seemed to have a connection with her cows. I don't know if it is actually a memory or just a sense of what I felt; but she seemed to know what the cows needed and even said hello and goodbye to them as though they understood.

She had a chicken coop. I remember this chicken coop not having any chickens. She explained to me that they egg would be kept in this coop and then chicks would hatch. I think there were eggs, but I don't recall. I have a strong memory of running around the front of her home on this farm in Oregon. I was running not from anything but to the house where everyone was. I ran straight through a spider web! I remember feeling terrified and tangled in the mess of the webs that clung to my little shoulders and arms. I was frightened thinking that there may be spiders all over me. It was then that my Great Grandmother Viola told me that spiders were magical creatures and that they would never harm me. My affinity with spiders began then and has only become more intense and magical over time. I don't have much more memory of my Great Grandmother's farm than this fragment here. I do remember one other time when she sat in the lawn with my sister and me and taught us how to braid daisies into our hair. Everything that I do remember about my Great Grandmother is magical. Her farm was special, her meals were incredible, and I felt a connection to her. She always remembered me when I saw her and seemed to just 'know' what was going on in my life.

My Great Grandmother was a writer. She wrote many beautiful things over her lifetime. I saw her another time at her birthday party. I believe it was her 96th. This time she had a walker. That didn't stop her. She ran all around that day and talked with everyone and had a grand old time. She and my Grandmother both spoke with me that day. My Great Grandmother reminisced about some incident involving beans that I don't recall now, and I don't think even then. My Grandmother scolded me about biting my nails and spoke of her most recent diabetes diagnosis and was disgruntled that she could not eat birthday cake. My last memory of her was in her little apartment in her nursing home. The farm now gone she lived in a small studio-like apartment.

I remember specifically that everything was very feminine. Lace and florals decorated her home and I remember floral china hanging on the wall. She had writings and books everywhere around her bed. She had a bout with disorientation due to a stroke, but she had her wits about her again and still spoke with me about my life. I don't remember specifics. I just remember a feeling I had about her. That she and I had a kinship of some kind and that somehow with my Great Grandma Viola; she understood me.

I didn't get to see my mom's side of the family very much. They lived in California and it was quite a big trip to go to see them. I saw my Grandmother on a couple occasions. The birthday party I spoke of, and a visit to her home in San Jose. I loved my Grandma too, I wish I had a better memory of her. I felt like she was always at a distance even when she did visit. She came once to our home in Iowa when I was a young adult. I remember it being pleasant but again distant. I think that part of this was the relationship my mother had with my grandmother. Although I know some about it; I don't know it all and wouldn't pretend to.

These two women have become an integral part of my healing; for me, my sister and my mother. These women carry the bloodline and the spiritual lineage that has been passed down now through many generations. This healing work began several years ago now. My mother, sister and I decided to open our Akashic records[22] for the three of us and the women in our family in order to bring healing and balance to our female lineage. The Akashic records are known to live in a place called the Hall of Records. The Hall of Records contains every soul's Book of Life. It contains within it; every lifetime, every contract, relationship, achievement and so on. There are guided meditations available to travel to the Akashic Records. There are some that believe only certain people

---

[22] In theosophy and anthroposophy, the **Akashic records** are a compendium of all human events, thoughts, words, emotions, and intent ever to have occurred in the past, present, or future. They are believed by theosophists to be encoded in a non-physical plane of existence known as the etheric plane. https://en.wikipedia. org/wiki/Akashic_records

are allowed to view their Book of Life. I don't believe that. It is my experience that anyone can follow the guided meditation and most have similar experiences. Everyone that I know who has tried has been able to connect with their Book of Life. Why would you want to look at it? You may be curious about a past life. You may wonder why you feel connected to a certain relationship. You may wonder how old your soul is or where you have been. There are lots of reasons. We chose to open our Book of Life to better understand our challenges as women; in relationships, health and our psychic gifts.

At the time, we enlisted the help of my trusted healer in the Bahamas. Opening the Akashic records is work you can do on your own. However, having non-bias support when channeling information is a benefit. Through the process we learned valuable information about our past lives. We learned that we had made commitments to break a vow of silence for the women in our lineage. For many lifetimes the women in our family hid their prophetic gifts from others. It was hiding those gifts out of fear that manifested physical issues within our genetics.

The Dalai Lama said; "If the mind is tranquil and occupied with positive thoughts, the body will not easily fall prey to disease."

It was my 'coming out' as a psychic in this lifetime that exposed our gifts. A profound change in this lifetime is that it is safe for me to share my gifts with the world. There is always judgement, but I will not be burned at the stake. My actions are showing not only my lineage, but many others out there who have held back their gifts -

It is safe to be your authentic self.

By understanding how karma, and the imprints from the minds of our lineage, affect our genetics and our health we were able to clear karmic residue. We had no idea the undertaking, nor the impact this would have on all three of us over the months following. This decision created incredible breakthroughs; not only in our relationships with each other and our health but laid down a path for my niece who was readying herself to embark on her own journey of life. For the first time in our lives together we were having open discussion about our gifts, sensitivities and beliefs. We were also looking at our physical health in a very real way and sharing our challenges. The work with the Akashic records brought us together as a female lineage. While the process was subtle, the healing to our family was profound and unified us where we had been separated.

Your Ancestral Foundation

Our values and morals created because of how we were raised is another ingredient to our Enlightenment Pie. Family. One could argue that it begins even before that; our Soul being the foundation of our very being. When I think of a foundation; I imagine the foundation of a house. The house itself could not stand without the cement foundation that roots it in the ground. Not only would the house falter but it would also not withstand the test of time, through storm and wind. I think it is the same for humans in the sense that we too have to have a solid foundation to stand on. Without it, we may be unable to withstand our own storms as we move through life. Most of us grow up with some kind of family dynamic. We grow up being taught by our parents or our parental figures certain morals and values; a structure to life and to our belief system. This structure operates as an imprint in our system that guides us on how to react to others and to situations that are presented in our life.

Within this structure is an idea of 'right' and 'wrong'. Each individual may have a different idea of this. My 'right' may not be the 'right' of another but we still operate on a structure of morals and/or values that were taught to us since we were young. This imprint operates almost like a tour guide through life. This tour guide can help us when we are uncertain of which direction to go. Problems can arise when our basic imprint no longer fits the space we are in or who we are. The imprint then feels like a French tour guide who is leading you on a tour of Italy. They cannot speak the language, nor do they know which direction to go. It is in these moments that you must create your own set of morals, values and beliefs. This is the process of growing up and separating from your parents. It is also the process of increased awareness. When we find ourselves unable to answer the questions that have appeared in our life; we must search for answers. Some of us search for these answers within others; friends, lovers, colleagues. Others may search for answers in education or mentors. And finally, some too will look to a Guru, a spiritual master or a priest. I note here that in my experience; when we begin to turn to our spiritual teachers, ultimately, we find ourselves turning within for answers, asking our own Self.

An interesting twist to this imprint or belief system we carry is that this not only comes from our parents who raised us but also from their parents, and their parents' parents and so on. In fact, our lineage is a structure of morals, beliefs and values that is placed upon us simply because we are part of the lineage, part of the family tree. This became increasingly important to me over the course of my own healing. I found as I began to dig into my lineage there were gifts and also triggers that were carried through all of the women in my family. In looking back, I was able to discover more about myself and why I was 'made' to feel/react/experience things in a certain way.

Our lineage directly impacts our present-day experience. By understanding our heritage, we understand ourselves.

I feel we must understand our moral and ancestral foundation in order to heal. By learning about where we came from, we begin to understand who we are. Even more healing is learning to embrace your family and your heritage and allow it to work for you rather than against you. Understanding your past brings you a greater awareness of your present. This brings healing to you and to your family; seven generations back and seven generations forward.

Going Home

> *"You leave home. You move on. You do the best you can.*
> *I got lost in this whole world and forgotten who I am."*
> *The House that Built Me Miranda Lambert*

Home. Nothing more perfect to describe home than Apple Pie. It is a symbol for the American family and in the Midwest, where I grew up, it's home. The smell of cinnamon and apples baking in the oven. The taste of a flaky crust with a hint of sugar. Vanilla ice cream melting into a creamy soup at the base of a perfect piece of apple pie. Soft apples melting in your mouth and with each bite filling with the essence of... home, summer, fireflies, the smell of the cornfields...

I grew up in small town Iowa. Now, if anyone asks, I will tell them I was born in Denver, CO and a short 7-year stint in Iowa. I'm laughing as I write this because I don't know many people that are proud of being from Iowa. Most of us find it difficult to admit. And yet, secretly inside, we love it. We love the simple pleasures that can be found on a farm or deep in the corn fields. There's something romantic about the changing colors of the Mississippi River in the fall. We love that we know absolutely everyone in town and that our favorite bartenders know us, and we know them...sometimes a little too well. Growing up in Iowa created many memories for me. Some good and some not so good. Although I have lived in Colorado for over 30 years now; Iowa is still my home and the place I 'go back' to when I need to find myself.

As we go through our journey of healing and self-discovery I am finding that we move closer to our Selves; who we were before...before we met the world. This journey has led me back to my childhood. It has led me back to who I was; before the big city, before marriage, career and debt. It came to me a during my illness that it was time to go home. Time for me to visit my childhood and my adolescent years and re-connect with who I was. The more in tuned I had become with who I was, the more connected I felt to that young gal who spent her time in the backwoods of the Iowa countryside. When I first started writing this section; I was planning a 10-day pilgrimage home. They say; the journey is the destination. The journey home is 836 miles of driving to my hometown. It is a trip into my heart, into the past, into relationships that broke me and connections that healed me; my childhood, my parents' divorce, my first love...much is lost and gained when you are young. There are many imprints...pictures of the past that have made us who we are. My sense today is that in order to fully heal you must face the past, bringing it into the present so you can truly create your life from where you stand… not from where you stood.

"On the road again…turn the page…" Willy Nelson

An empty hotel room in the middle of Nebraska; the wind from my open car window still ringing in my ears. A thunderstorm rolling into town. The first few drops fall on the window pane like large stones a child had thrown. The storm lets loose. In a matter of moments, the clouds open up and rain is pouring down; filling the streets with water and lightning flashing through the night sky. A sense of relief hits me as I know I just made it here before the storm hit. I watch the rainfall and the lightning flash. I look out to the parking lot full of cars and the small country dive that happens to be next door. There are all sorts of people at this hotel in Kearney. Some folks are here with their horse trailers; I can only imagine coming or going to or from a county fair. There are station wagons; the dreaded family trip, and there are other cars like mine. Perhaps other single folks taking a simple journey from one place to another. We all somehow ended up here in this tiny Rodeway Inn in the middle of nowhere.

It was a beautiful drive out of Colorado. Not a cloud in the sky. Although this summer night was hot it was cool in comparison to the heat of the day and made for a comfortable drive out of town. I watched the thunderheads in the distance for a couple of hours hoping they would not cross my path. As soon as I crossed the border out of Colorado and into Nebraska I noticed the sudden change in scenery. For miles and miles all you can see are cornfields. There are occasional spots along various rivers and creeks where trees have grown. They are like small Oasis' in the middle of nowhere. The corn is tall this year. Everything is so green. It is beautiful in its own way. The farmhouses and silos speckle the land and the occasional John Deere tractor is plowing one field or another. It may sound silly but there are two favorite things on this drive to see. The first is a large cattle farm in the middle of Nebraska. There are literally hundreds of cows all in one spot. Since I was 9 years old I have driven by that cattle farm. There is something to it. It reminds me of something; although I'm not sure what. My second favorite thing is the large sprinkler systems used to water the fields. I love watching them spray water back and forth across acres of corn or soybeans. It reminds me of summer and is one of the things that stayed the same.

I've driven this stretch of highway hundreds of times before. Many important events in my life were shared with this stretch of I-80; high school graduation, college, my first bad break up, and my second. I've shed tears on this road. I've spilt blood on this road. I've felt my heart on this road. I've laughed on this road and felt anticipation too. Pain... fear...love...joy...all emotions that this asphalt has carried. It holds a lot of energy for me. Between living in Iowa and Colorado and family in both states I have gone back and forth more times than I can count. Ogallala, North Platte, Kearney, Grand Island, Lincoln, Omaha, Des Moines, Cedar Rapids...the trek home is memorized and could be driven with eyes closed. Some trips have been amazing; beautiful weather, fall leaves, springtime budding...starting a new life, meeting a love. Other trips have been not so amazing; hot and sticky, sweaty summer heat, white out/white knuckle blizzards...leaving love behind, saying goodbye to old friends. The journey home is always a pilgrimage in itself. The 12-hour drive oftentimes is therapeutic. It provides the much-needed time alone to contemplate life's great mystery. On many of my trips home I have looked forward to the time in the car. I play music, sing and think. It clears my head and my space in preparation for another stage of my life.

As I am writing this now, a thought comes; isn't it synchronistic that we happen to 'go home' when we are going through a change in our life? What is it that home creates? Home is safe. Home feels comfortable. If home is our security and our safety net to make big decisions, changes or to 'clean up' who we are; how do we create 'home' wherever we are? How can we provide ourselves with that safety net when there is no home? Or at least no place that feels like home. I think of Dorothy and the Wizard of Oz...'there's no place like home...' So true, and yet; isn't home where the heart is? Why would I leave my heart in Iowa? In my past? Why would any of us leave our heart behind? I am reminded of Osho who speaks of the tortoise. The tortoise carries his home with him wherever he goes. "Now is the time to come home to yourself…"

The music played on my IPOD all night. Each song holds a special memory for me and in many cases the music brought me back; back to the road. The road home is not a simple stretch of highway. It is not the music that plays or the summer thunderstorms that lead you there. It is a road 'home to your Self'. It is a journey back to who you are. Everything that we have experienced is what has built us. Our life's adventures are what make us. Going 'home' is remembering where you came from, what you have come through, and where you are…so you can 'see' yourself.

When I arrived in my hometown I decided to drive the small country highway to the small town I grew up in. The highway is only two lane and it has never changed. Most of the homes along the way were still the same, although a bit more run down. About 20 minutes into the drive I came upon the curve where my mom, brother and I had a car accident. It happened many years ago now. We hit black ice and rolled our Ram Charger three times, smashing into a massive oak tree. We were very lucky to have survived with minimal injury. It was winter, and my memory of that accident is broken into pieces now. I remember watching the ditch come close and then far as we skidded back and forth. The next thing I knew I was face down in the snow. I couldn't remember how I got there. I also remember feeling upset that I was there. Even now, I think that I had left my body when I was unconscious and perhaps didn't want to come back. They say you have to have a near death experience to open your trans-medium channels. I think this was that experience for me. Here I was; coming conscious and staring at the SUV upside down and my mom hanging by her seatbelt asking if I was okay. It is summer as I drove by that tree now. You would never know that something like that had happened so long ago.

My home growing up was in a rural neighborhood about 10 miles outside of a very little Iowa town. There are three very distinct hills on the main road back to my old neighborhood. My goodness how many times we went up and down those hills each day to school! As I went over the third and final hill I was shocked at how much the neighborhood had changed. There were houses where meadows used to be, and our bus house was long gone. The parents had all chipped in to build a small shed of a house at our bus stop to shield us from the weather. I cannot tell you how many times my wet hair froze when it hit the frigid winter air. We used to huddle in that bus house; even though most of us did not get along, just to stay warm until that bus arrived. When I came upon my childhood home I felt the emotions welling up inside of me. Nostalgic energy is very curious. It makes you very emotional and yet you really aren't sure why. Memories flood into your mind and you are overcome. I parked on the road near the driveway and started to walk. I was hopeful no one would stop me wondering who I was. Looking at the expansive driveway, I remembered how my dad had poured that huge driveway, so we could roller-skate and play basketball. We skated every day for years on that driveway. There were houses directly next door to the house now, on three sides. When I grew up here it was all just forest. I saw the edge of the yard where the forest line still stood.

Behind that line was a small trail that led back to the oak tree. The oak tree had been there all my childhood. It was a tree that had fallen after being struck by lightning. All of my adolescence was spent writing on that oak tree. I walked to the back of the yard. The trail was long gone. I walked through what was likely poison ivy and moss and thick forest to get back to the creek. The oak tree was gone! I couldn't believe it. I had hoped to re-connect with that tree and that writing space. But alas it was gone. I sat there, Creekside, as though I was in mourning for a lost soul. All of the moments of building forts on that tree and picking at the moss and bark on that tree flipped through my mind's eye. After a few more moments I walked back to my car. I had remembered what I needed to. I saw the reflections of my past. It was time to head back into town.

The rest of that trip was more mundane than that day at the creek. It was visiting family and seeing old friends. Going home allowed me to re-connect with my parents and to pull old memories out of stores I had forgotten. I had many insights on that trip and continued to document them in my journal. You may be so lucky as to journey back to your childhood home. You may not. I hope you have old journals or photos to help you sift through your memories. The goal is to remember who you were; before the world changed you. Once you have spent time in your keepsake box, re-living memories of your childhood, and examining your relationship with your parents; it is time to go back even further. Now you must journey into your lineage. By coming to understand your ancestors; you will understand even more about yourself.

Healing Your Etheric DNA/Generational Healing

"I seem to recognize your face
Haunting familiar here
I can't seem to place it
Can I find a candle of thought
To light your name
Lifetimes are catchin' on with me." Pearl Jam

There are so many experiences I have had throughout my healing that led me to my ancestors and to the women that are now such an integral part of my journey. How strange it is that the last place I looked for answers were within my own family heritage. You would think it would be the place to begin. It is why I am talking about the journey here now. Looking back, into the past, is precisely what propels you forward. By peeling back, the layers of our past, we come to terms with our present and then seem suddenly able to move forward with a clarity that was not there before. When we look back at ourselves and our family, as an adult, we gain a new perspective. It is from the heights of the new perspective that we 'see' clearly who we are and where we came from.

I am reminded of a message that came up several times over the last few years. I purchased a 'psychic circle' board[23] a few years back. The board

---

[23] Psychic Circle https://www.amazon.com/Psychic-Circle-Magical-Message-Board/dp/0671866451

is very similar to the Oija board but is bright colored and somehow feels safe and more positive than the associated energies of the old school Oija board. In this board it has several symbols or images on it that the divining tool can cross over. Several times I received the same message…the hot air balloon. The message states: "What you know of your situation is incomplete unless you rise above it and take in the whole picture. You may be excluding vital facts because you are too close to the situation. Make some breathing room. Beware of obsessive thinking in yourself as well as in others. One must take the risks to gain perspective. To stay where you are is safe, but there is less opportunity for growth. Fear of failure stops many from trying to soar. Once the whole picture is seen, actions can be undertaken. These actions will not be understood by those whose view is not as privileged. Once you determine to see all there is to see, you must be ready to accept the accompanying emotional upheaval. If it threatens to stop your vision quest, you must practice emotional detachment."

This message is extremely powerful today. At the time, I thought I understood it and perhaps I did to a certain extent. I am certain a few years from now I will see a new perspective that is different even from today. To gain perspective is to gain awareness, to expand your consciousness. It only makes sense that when being asked to gain perspective into yourself and your life; you must pull your vision back and look at where you came from. Taking a look into your lineage, your heritage and your ancestors can bring to light talents, handicaps and a greater understanding of your own choices throughout your life. Gaining perspective is not just about looking into your ancestors but also looking into your own past. Where have you been? What has brought you to this point, this place where you are today?

Whether we like it or not; we are our family. We carry their bloodline and more, so we carry the many genetic traits the line has within it. Our level of intelligence, our ability to connect with others, our creativity, our eating habits, our emotions; these are all pieces of the ancestral 'pie'. A student said to me, "I'm afraid if I look back; I will not be able to come out of it and move forward." I think this is a fear in all of us. If we open up Pandora's box, will we be able to liberate ourselves from it? Or will we get stuck in the muck that it has created and be unable to achieve our authentic selves? I think the answer to this is that we must go back. We must dig into what created us. Our family, how we were raised, and who was around us as children, are what molds us. The energy of our family shapes us into young adults. Our lineage, our bloodline, provides the framework of who we are. To liken it to a pie; our lineage is the flour in the makings of the crust and our experiences with our family in this life as young children, is the butter that holds the flour in place.

What do you do with this? How do you begin to investigate our ancestry? I think it begins by understanding your own experience of growing up and furthermore, developing an understanding of your relationship with your family in the present. I believe a great place to begin is coming to understand your relationship with your parents. Who influenced you the most? Your Mom? Your Dad? How have each of them impacted you and your life? If you were to look back at your early years of childhood, from as early as you remember to about 12; who were you closest with? Do you remember the first time you felt resentment towards your parents? Do you remember the time they were most proud? When did you feel understood by your parents? Have you ever felt understood?

I'm certain there was a time where you felt very connected to your parents. You may not have liked the connection. It may have been the time you realized you were just like your mother, or that time you handled a situation exactly like your father. There may be times for some of you where you remember a closeness with your parents and are thankful for their protection. There are others reading this who may have wanted protection from their parents and the abuse laid upon you by them. I encourage you to do an activity and complete the self-inquiry questions. This activity should only take an hour or so to complete although much more may come up over time.

Activity 1. From a seated position, go into meditation. If you are not familiar with a meditation practice, just sit quietly and breathe deeply until you feel your mind is quieted. Then reach into the filing cabinets of your memory and pull out the last time you saw your parents. You can focus this exercise on your mother or your father or both, whichever feels right to you.

Journal Entry

What was it like the last time you saw them?

How did you feel? What was the energy?

What was the conversation like?

Then dig into the filing cabinet again and look at the first time you remember feeling resentment towards your parent(s). What happened?

What do you remember about that time? How did you feel? How did they react?

Then take yourself back to a time you remember your parent(s) feeling proud of you? What was the achievement? How did they make you feel?

Go back further yet into your memory file to the time when you were an infant. Although you may not remember specifics; how did you feel as a baby? What was your relationship with your parents? What is your sense about that time? Were you happy? Were your parents happy?

Lastly, take yourself back into the womb. What was it like to be in your mother's belly? How did you feel? How did your mother feel? Take some deep cleansing breaths and journal your experience.

It can be a powerful experience to go back in time and take a look at the memories that rise to the surface. If asked we can pull many memories out of our file from our childhood. But there is a choice few that really stay with us. There are many others we forget. We either block them out of our mind completely or we simply just don't remember them as important. It's interesting the shreds of the past that can take us into a place we did not remember. Just recently I was going through my keepsakes from the past and I stumbled upon old writings from different years of school. As I read them I was amazed that I had written them. The thought that went into the writing surprised me. I don't even really remember writing them down and yet here they were, in my own handwriting. I also saw pictures I drew and poems I wrote.

One of the most fascinating pieces I found was a drawing I had done in 2nd grade. It was pictures of many witches and ghosts flying in the air. I even drew a black cat on the broom handle of one of the witches flying and ghosts coming in through an open window. There was a story I had written attached to this drawing.

"One night it was blowing so hard! I couldn't go trick or treating at all. But we went anyway.

We saw an old house. We went inside it was gloomy.
Witches on broomsticks gosh I was scared. It turned out we were at home. The End"

I love this story even reading it now! The relevance of this is quite incredible and I immediately began to psychoanalyze the meanings behind it as soon as I read it. How interesting that I had written about witches at all! I wondered if it was a project for Halloween for school. I don't have a memory of it. To write so clearly about witches flying on broomsticks and then to summarize the story with the revelation we were actually at home. Was I saying that home was actually with these witches? That the occult was my home? I wonder. In addition to this drawing and story there were several other witches I had drawn, cut out, or created that were saved in this keepsake box. At the time this was certainly an intriguing piece of evidence pointing to my psychic abilities and connections to the occult realm at such a young age. Looking around at my home there is no mistake that I was once consumed by witches and the idea of witchcraft.

I have another memory of going to the shopping mall as a young girl of 10 and 11. Because we lived in rural Iowa at the time, it was a good hour drive to the city from our home. It was a special bi-monthly occasion. My little brother and I were always given allowance money to keep us entertained while my parents ran their errands. While my little brother went straight to the arcade; I went to the bookstore. I have strong memory recollection of several occasions over many months that I would sit in the New Age section of the bookstore thumbing through books about the occult. I even still own a few of the 'spell books' I purchased during that time. They serve as a reminder of where I began my journey into spiritual understanding. In looking back at the books on the shelf and the pictures in my box of keepsakes; I wonder how I could be so consumed with the idea of witches and just forget? How does that happen? This is why I feel there is such an importance in investigating your childhood and your past. There may be many things that you forgot over time. It's amazing to me thinking about it even now, that we can go so far from ourselves and yet we also find our way back. To explain further; although I do not remember spending so much time involving myself with the occult or the idea of witchcraft, it still became an integral part of my life. As a 19-year-old I found myself drawn back to my Tarot Cards I had learned a few years before with my mother. In my mid-twenties I found myself again drawn to the Craft of the Wise and to Wicca. This desire to connect with this nature driven, pagan lifestyle or philosophy was/is inherent within me. Why? It is this question and trying to understand myself that I began to dig deeper into my heritage. Even after journeying into the past and shedding light on my connection with the occult; I still found myself surprised when finding this story of writing about witches in the end being 'home'. I did not realize that it was in fact also going to become a huge piece of the ancestral karma that, with the help of my mother and sister, I would begin to heal.

The point of this drawn out description of my discovery of the past, is that we must look back in order to understand ourselves. I can only hope we are all so lucky as to have a parent who decided to keep everything we wrote, every report card we had and every assignment we turned in. We may not be so lucky, and we may have to dig into our memories or even talk with our family about who we were. There are resources available to us to look at our past. We have to seek those resources out, open the keepsake boxes or dig into the attic to discover our truth as we knew it in our youth. Once we have opened the box we then need to take in that person that we were. We said things and we made choices. We put our energy into our passions while we discarded what we didn't understand or like. It is in our youth that we most understood where we had come from most recently; I speak here of our past lives if you believe in reincarnation. And whether you believe in reincarnation or not, I hope you agree that in our youth we are not imprinted with the many things the world has to offer, both good and bad. Instead we carry with us an innocence. We are not necessarily tied to what people think or what we 'should' or 'should not' do. Instead we understand a basic idea of right and wrong and we figure out, through inquiry (either in action or in words) what we can 'get away with'. It is over time and with experience that we understand the lines and begin to formulate conclusions about how the world works.

As an adult, after years of 'imprinting'; we can look back on that innocent time and begin to understand the root of ourselves. I believe this root is the inner child spoken of in so many psychology books. Our inner child, I believe, is that innocent piece of ourselves that was only connected to ourselves. That child that had not yet been hurt and that had not yet been told no. Our inner child is that piece of our soul that remains untouched. That child knows what it loves and what it doesn't. He or She knows exactly why she came here, his/her purpose and how she is going to achieve it. Each child is different in how they connect with others and what they are drawn naturally to. For me, I was always writing. I remember each time it would rain how excited I would become. I would grab my notepad and go to the that large oak tree behind my home and write poetry or thoughts in the rain. It seems such an odd thing now looking back. I still don't understand what was driving me to sit in the rain and write. Especially at such a young age; I remember being as young as ten years old. To this day I love the sound of the crackling of paper after it has dried from being wet. I love the smell of the rain and of course I still love to write. That emotion or feeling has stayed with me all these years, all my life. What a strange nostalgia? Even at a young age it was a nostalgic feeling, this great love to sit in the rain. And where does this nostalgia come from? Another life perhaps? A fond memory that I have lost to time? I'm not certain even now. I think we each have those memories. These odd memories from our childhood experience that are still with us. That are part of us and even though our minds and bodies have gone through the test of time; we still, for some reason, have this built in 'stuff' that is our authentic self.

Our authentic self has always been there. We must expand our vision of our life to gain perspective on our life. In looking back, we are actually looking across the entirety of our life. This helps us to then link those moments of happiness and success. These moments reveal our purpose.

It was only after reviewing old ACT scores and several years of report cards that the message was clear. Lisa should be a writer when she 'grows up'. Did I really need to wait until a third of my life was over to receive affirmation that I should in fact write? Take the time to look back and across. It will reveal much about who you are and what direction you should go. Complete the following activity and self-inquiry questions. This may take an afternoon or as long as a full week. It really depends on how long it takes you to process through what information you are receiving.

Activity 2: Write down the names of your ancestors and their date of birth going back seven generations. You can do only the female side or only the male side or both depending on what you feel you need to work on. Meditate on those names. You can even light a candle and ask those ancestors to come in to your space. If you have pictures of them put them up as a mandala to meditate on them. Place your left palm on Mother Earth. Invite your spirit guide, ancestor teachers and/or Spirit into the right palm facing upwards. Ask to please remove the genes from the ancestor that are blocking you or affecting you adversely and feel them release into the Earth. Notice what you feel and note them here.

Journal Entry

Create a prayer or affirmation around your lineage. What do you want
to heal? What do you want to know?

7

Food Addiction and Parasites

I'd like to go back now to 2011 and the time I first met my doctor and was awaiting test results to find out what was wrong with me. It had been six months since I fell ill. My inner transformation had been intense, and the outer has followed suit. My routine changed, friends changed, my work changed...so much change. A move to a smaller apartment and a possible change in my job also presented itself during this time. After months of chanting, prayer and practice I had brought myself back into balance and into a healthier state. But I couldn't stop there. The transformation was not yet complete. Although I had given up wheat, dairy, soy and gluten; in addition, I added a more disciplined meditation and chanting practice – with all of this; there was still more to let go.

"We will part from each of the loved ones we have long befriended.
We will leave behind the wealth we have so diligently amassed.
Our consciousness, the guest, will cast away
this body, the guest-house." Shantideva

This segment from Shantideva's, *A Bodhisattva's Way of Life* overwhelmed me with emotion the first time I read it. I was in Radio City Music Hall in New York City. I attended a three-day teaching with His Holiness the Dalai Lama. At the end of the three days he offered anyone who wanted to take Refuge Vows and the Bodhisattva Vow; to do so with Him. As I read the phrases from the book this particular phrase was incredibly profound. I had in fact cast away my body as I knew it. I was in fact alone. I had left many friendships behind and even my marriage in my pursuit of balance and health. This was a turning point in my life. At this critical point in my journey of transformation I wondered where I go from here.

What happens after you become balanced and healthy?
How do you stay disciplined when you re-
insert yourself back into your life?

These two questions are not only valid but present a significant challenge. One that I am still processing through, and one that we all ultimately must face in one way or another. When we are well and 'feeling good' we tend to forget all the times we 'felt bad' or sick or suffered in some way. Once we make it through the terrible flight or the horrible illness; what then? Do we only pray when we need it most? Are we only thankful for receiving an answer to our prayers in the moment? Moments are fleeting. Life is ever-changing; and yet, there is one thing that we should not change - our practice.

Let me begin first by speaking of my journey with food. I grew up in a family that loved to cook and certainly loved to eat. I was blessed that my parents took us on trips all over the country and were always creating openings for new experiences. Half the fun of traveling or the holidays, or even a Sunday night, is what you are eating. After graduating high school, I decided to go to Culinary School. Becoming the proverbial foodie was no problem for me. My love of food and of cooking made culinary school a breeze. I even married a chef. Living with a chef is a marvelous thing, especially when he is a good one. I would come home to rack of lamb or roasted chicken, caviar and sometimes lobster. He could take anything that was in the pantry and turn it into a work of art. Once a week we ventured all over town to new restaurants, old ones and dives in between. After 8 years of indulgence I put on nearly 100 pounds. Certainly, a piece of the gain was the unknown food allergies and the consistent eating out and eating processed foods. But, another piece of the weight gain was baggage and addiction.

I have a history of toxic relationships both plutonic and romantic. Watching another person continually make poor choices during a relationship gave me permission to feed my own destructive patterns. It wasn't until I was faced with the possibility of dying that I finally changed my ways with food and actually faced the mirror I had been ignoring for so long. Food addiction is not any easier to deal with than addiction to drugs or alcohol. Ultimately our addiction is filling some kind of void or emptiness. There is something that we do not want to face or some part of ourselves we don't want to see. And so, we self-medicate. At the end of a stressful week I felt entitled to that piece of chocolate cake just as much as an addict may feel entitled to a tall cold beer. And so, my relationships enabled me. My partners of my past allowed us to be out of control in our own unique way and didn't face what was right in front of us. Both of us were full of discontent.

After leaving each toxic relationship I would drop 20 pounds almost immediately. Just leaving the environment shifted enough energy to give way to some of the excess baggage. I would return to my trail and walking 3 miles every day and certainly being single changes ones eating habits. At first the walking was always painful. My hips were sore, and my body ached. Even my feet hurt. At 30 years old I really shouldn't have been that out of shape. But I was. After about 6 months of walking and eating for one, I lost 30 total pounds and was feeling much better. It wasn't until I was completely depleted of energy and in a near dying state that I actually truly faced what food and my addiction to it, had been doing to me all these years. With no other options and the Doctors orders to go to a completely clean diet while my test results were processing; I began a journey into the one mirror I hadn't been able to face.

Addiction.

After a week without caffeine, sugar, wheat, gluten, dairy or even fruit; I began to understand how a crack addict must feel when they first begin withdrawals from their substance. The night sweats, the shakiness, the cravings. It was extremely difficult. I was also completely exhausted.

I had been feeding my body with caffeine and sugar for 32 years. My doctor had warned me that my adrenal glands would go through upheaval. After years of being overworked by caffeine, they were now forced to function on their own. The first 7 days I experienced Adrenal crashing. Essentially you have no energy and feel as though you cannot do anything but sleep. I spent most of the time I was awake chanting or praying. I did try to walk on my trail behind my home but could only go about halfway before I needed to rest. If I ventured out of the house I was bombarded by all of the things I couldn't have; the smell of Starbucks and fast food restaurants. Even passing through certain favorite aisles at the grocery store was torture. Only allowed to eat green, alkaline vegetables and protein made it extremely difficult to eat anywhere. Not only was I unable to fill my body with the substances that it craved, but I also had my social scene completely eliminated. Unable to go out and with no energy to do it; I was at home every day and every night with my addiction. Each time I had to cook for myself I was forced to face the fact that I was starving and that nothing that I was able to put into my body was what I wanted. Even fresh vegetables and chicken tasted poor and was unsatisfying. This is when I had my first awareness of my addiction.

What was it I was really craving?
Why was I not satisfied?
What was this experience teaching me?

For the first time in my life I was realizing that the toxicity that had been facing me every day was a mirror reflection of my own inner toxicity. I knew at that time that I had to face myself and the baggage I was carrying that led to this addiction. They say in AA that the first step is admitting you have a problem. Anyone who has been there understands that there truly is a pivotal moment where you do finally 'see' that you have an addiction and that it has taken over your life. You also finally come to terms with the fact that it has been destroying your health and your life. This is quite a lot to process. It took me another couple of weeks just to understand the realization and awakening that was occurring just from seeing my own Self differently. I also realized how I had made so many judgements regarding others faults when in actuality they were my own.

After the awareness of my addiction; I then had to ask myself why? Why did I need food? What was it doing for me? Now this process of self-inquiry was all fine and good, but I must share that in the midst of all of this I had been forced to go cold turkey off of all my 'normal' foods to save my health. Because my body was getting stronger every day I was able to move through the withdrawals. What was replacing the outer illness was an inner loneliness that I couldn't ignore.

How many of us really take care of ourselves? How many of us go to the organic section of the grocery store and pick the best vegetables and the highest quality meats? And how many of us take the time to cook them to perfection and season them with high quality fats and seasonings and then serve ourselves? To take it further, how many of us then pray before we eat and give our food humbly over to those in need? How many of us ask our bodies to process our food properly and to take great care of what we are putting in our body, putting it to our best possible use? How many of us think of the sacrifices made to bring this food to us? How many of us every put that much thought into what we eat?

Most of us are on the go. Life is busy and full. We grab and go. We run through drive-thrus. We run into the grocery store and grab something pre-made to heat up in our microwave. We have dishwashers to wash the dishes we rarely use and the space that is most used in any kitchen is typically the garbage can – filled with empty fast food paper bags and leftovers no one would eat. Makes us feel kind of sick doesn't it?

Preparing the few foods I could eat in my kitchen and hoping that they did not make me sick was a daily practice after 3 weeks of the candida diet. Still no word on my test results. I had extreme anxiety about everything I put into my body. Having no idea what was causing me to be sick I was overcome with panic anytime something didn't sit right. In addition, I was back at work and getting through the day was like scratching nails down a chalkboard. It hurt and was uncomfortable and you wanted to get away, but you couldn't. It took every single bit of energy I had to get through the day and with only spinach salads and hard-boiled eggs to get me through the day...well, it was rough. No caffeine and no quick fix made work very difficult. I worked in an industry where you are constantly moving and on the go. This was not conducive for healing and taking time for self-care. I went home every night and could barely get through cooking a dinner before I had to just go to sleep. I chanted when I made all of my meals. I listened to Kuan Yin chants[24] each morning and cooked my breakfast. I thanked all of my meals for taking care of me. All of my energy was channeled into feeding myself. It was quite intense. I had to think about everything I ate before I ate it. I had to think about where it came from and how it was prepared. I essentially bought and made everything myself as there was no way to trust what was made elsewhere. I slept and cooked and ate.

In addition, I still had some strange symptoms going on. I became jaundice and had some liver issues going on that were affecting my mood and also my body. I just kept pressing on. The Universe has quite a unique way of guiding us though - if we listen. I remember being concerned about pulling through all this. The diet was helping and yet there were so many other random and subtle issues lingering. My altar or puja at the time was a bookshelf with all my spiritual books on it. An antique Buddhist altar was on top of the bookshelf with various assorted things piled on it; my rosary, sage, candles and incense and statues and pictures of spirits and deities and Gurus I had come to know and love. On this particular night I sat praying in front of my altar. Suddenly a Tao chanting book[25] fell off my shelf! It landed on the floor and the page opened to a Tao Liver Chant. Well you are darn straight that I started chanting that chant every day. Slowly but surely, I got stronger and stronger. After almost exactly 30 days of the candida diet and hours and hours of chanting; I suddenly felt awake.

---

[24] Namo Guan Shi Yin Pusa https://youtu.be/ONE8CNd7mt4

[25] Master Sha Tao II https://www.amazon.com/Tao-II-Rejuvenation-Longevity-Immortality-ebook/dp/B003UYURX8/ref=pd_sim_351_1?_encoding=UTF8&psc=1&refRID=VXYFTP9A7G8W09HG9ZBV

It was like coming out of a dream. One morning I awoke and had energy. I felt good. I made my breakfast and could really taste the food. Suddenly the vegetables I had been forcing down my throat for a month were tasting incredibly. It was like my sense of taste was re-born. I also had energy again. Almost all the symptoms I had had with my illness; headache, sinus pain, swelling, exhaustion, were gone. I also noticed that my life long insomnia had disappeared, and I was sleeping full nights. A rash I had on my chest for years was gone. I just all around felt better and clearer. I had overcome the cravings and the substances that I had long been addicted to. It may not have been cocaine or alcohol, but still just as difficult and devastating to my health. I imagine that this is how anyone else who has dealt with overcoming an addiction has felt once the substances were finally free from the body. You feel free. Freedom.

After 6 very long weeks of waiting I finally received my test results. I have to admit that after 6 weeks on the candida diet I was feeling overall very well. I still had some energy issues and sometimes felt off track, but I was really coming back into myself. I remember that I was supposed to get my test results on a Friday. They didn't come. I was bummed. The old and 'normal' reaction would have been to throw a tantrum of some kind and be totally impatient. And oh yeah, throw my cards a few hundred times to verify an answer. But that part of me had shifted over the course of 45 days of clean eating and Tao chanting. I remembered one of my teachers telling me that I need to learn to be in my process. And I took that very seriously. I decided not to look at it psychically. I decided to be in my process. For that weekend I continued to focus on healthy eating and I took walks out on my trail. I continued my process. I knew after all these months of being ill and being completely in the dark about my body I would finally have a real answer.

Parasites and 22 food allergies were my answer. I had three different parasites wreaking havoc on my body. One in my liver that could have destroyed it. Even my doctor commented on the power of the Tao chant I was doing and how that very well could have helped salvage my liver. I was allergic to wheat and severe allergy to dairy. There were many others but those are the big ones. I was going to have to change my diet forever, but I wouldn't have to live with those parasites forever. A simple combination of holistic herbs would kill those suckers and continue to starve them out by staying on the candida diet and eliminating sugar. My doctor and I both were thrilled that we had data and news and that I was healing rapidly because of my dedication to the diet and the practice given to me.

I did take time to savor that moment…but only for a moment. As one layer of baggage was leaving me, another layer of loneliness and grief had been building up inside me. I wasn't able to go out in fear I would consume something that would make me ill. I also still was quite tired in the evening and having no energy meant I wasn't even able to see friends in my apartment or in their home. My life had quite literally become work each day and resting each night. It felt as though I had left the world in some way. I wasn't able to participate in the many things that we tend to fill our lives with…drinking, coffee shops, bars, restaurants. All of these were pleasant social distractions from any piece of our daily life we don't want to face. Forced out of these spaces meant I had to sit at home with just me.

"Loneliness is the absence of the other. Aloneness is the presence of Oneself." Osho[26]

I love this quote. Not only is it beautiful but it is quite poignant. When you feel lonely, you are missing those that were once in your life. Your deceased pet, your ex-partner, your friends or colleagues. You feel empty and this leads to despair. Aloneness is feeling full with only yourself. It is about being present with yourself and allowing you to be enough. When are we ever enough? It was difficult to leave my marriage. My husband had been my best friend for almost 13 years and our home with my step daughter and our pets was always busy and full of people. You never were alone. There were certainly times when you wished you were,

---

[26] Osho Zen Tarot https://www.amazon.com/Tarot-Spirit-Zen-Osho-ebook /dp/B005BP0ED2/ref=sr_1_2?s=digital-text&ie=UTF8&qid=15238 11778&sr=1-2&keywords=Osho+zen+tarot+cards

but the idea was a luxury. By the time I had gotten ill, I had been living alone for two years. In those two years I had filled my work and social calendar with so much activity that I never had a moment to myself. In addition to changing my eating habits I had also been forced to change my social habits. It wasn't until I realized how lonely I was that I recognized that not only had I been addicted to certain food substances, but I was also addicted to a certain level of social interaction. I never woke up and got out of bed on my own. I would get on the phone or on my computer. Facebook had replaced reading books and YouTube videos replaced television. Going to a bar with a friend replaced companionship and dating had replaced intimacy. Not only was my illness forcing me to create a whole different way of eating but of living altogether. Nothing could be the same. Going back to old habits was truly impossible. In this awareness, I knew it I needed to admit to myself how lonely I was. I had to look at how I had risked myself to hide from my loneliness.

Parasites

Parasites are defined as an animal or plant that lives on another organism. The metaphysical reflection of the parasites;

I had allowed everyone to 'feed' off of my energy for their own sakes and for my loneliness' sake.

I started to integrate what parasites really meant for me. I wondered; how much of our own energy, body and self are we willing to give to another to ensure that we are not alone? I do believe that the parasites were brought upon me by my own soul. I believe that my spirit had decided my current choice of distractions was enough. I was giving everything of myself away to others in order to maintain a level of distraction from who I was or what I really was going through. I am thankful every single day to those little bugs as they changed the relationship I have with; food, my body, with the friends I have and myself.

After the treatment of the parasites and by remaining off of gluten, wheat and dairy in addition to all 22 of my allergies; I was not only healthy, but I had lost another 50 pounds. I was now 85 pounds lighter than I was when I left my marriage. And within those 85 pounds I lost baggage as well. The literal weight that my poor little body had been carrying was filled with emotional weight. Weight from addiction, loneliness, grief, anger, depression, and loss. As all of this fell away I felt lighter – in all aspects. It had now been over 6 months since I had first gotten ill and I was feeling strong and happy.

If you are not feeling really good each and every day, then you are already in the danger zone. There are already things happening within yourself that are not balanced or supporting your system. Our physical being is a mirror reflection of our emotional being. If we are unhappy, discontent, or uncertain about aspects in our life; it will reflect in our physical appearance or even in our chosen actions each day with others. Our reactions and our distractions influence all that we do. The first step is having the awareness that something is not right. It is seeing yourself – 'really seeing' – for who you are and how you look. There is a fine line we walk between feeling good about ourselves no matter what we look like and coming to terms with the fact that we are not healthy. There's nothing easy about any of this. But I want you to know that you can do it. You can make the changes you need to. You can look at yourself. You can become who you want to be. You can take that long hard look in the mirror and then step into it rather than turn your back to it.

The journey to complete health is not easy. It's not just about a diet or a prescription or even something being clearly wrong or an illness that is able to pinpoint. Complete health and vitality is really about feeling good. We have all had those days where we felt really good. We had energy, we were happy...but they are too few and far between. What would it be like to feel good every single day? What would it be like to wake up each morning with energy and to know that what you eat will make you stronger rather than wanting to take a nap? It is possible. When you think of your health at this time I want you to complete the following self-inquiry questions.

Journal Entry

Addiction.

What is it I am really craving?

Why am I not satisfied?

What is this experience teaching me?

Loneliness.

Am I lonely?

How am I feeding my loneliness?

Vitality.

When was the last time I felt really good? Physically? Emotionally? Mentally?

When was the last time I felt strong?

How often do I have the energy to exercise within my day? Even when I have to work?

How often do I feel really good even after eating a meal?

How often have I been sick with something in the last year? Cold etc.

8

Cutting into It

I sit at a coffee shop on Pearl St. in Boulder, CO. A woman stands in front of me speaking to a man about his political beliefs, clipboard in hand. I am certain she is taking a survey. A man playing with a yoyo caught my attention as I walked here. He seemed to be lost in his vision of the strings and moved the yoyo effortlessly from side to side. Businessmen in suits came into the shop and behind them a man on his cell phone with his backpack and cargo shorts. The diversity of people in this space is clear by the onlookers. Although I did not move more than an hour from my home of 15 years; I feel as though I have moved to a different country. Though this place is very different; it holds all of my energy here. My beliefs, my food habits, my love of community and diversity; it's all contained in this place called Boulder.

A chain of synchronistic events led me to this very different space. It has been 7 years since I received what you might name your 'calling' and 4 ½ years since I left my husband in search of myself. I barely remember who I was 7 years ago. I was unhappy, overweight, and lost. A couple of weeks ago, while I was packing to move to Boulder, I came across my keepsakes. A box of old things lost to this cardboard compartment. As I sorted through the many pictures and misc. pieces of paper; I realized I barely recognized the women in the pictures that was thought to be me. I feel as though my spirit was taken out of that body and placed in a different one. I now had a different career path, a different home, living in a different town, my body is different, my car is different, even my dishes in my kitchen are different. There is not much left of the woman I was. All I have are these random pictures, documenting where I have come from. Even in digging into my elementary school report cards; I almost don't recognize it. The only consistent string confirming that was in fact me are the comments written by the teachers confirming I should be a writer when I 'grow up'.

I moved to Boulder in June of 2012; one year after my recovery from parasites. I had decided to go back to school to get my bachelor's Degree and was going to attend Naropa University. I was excited about the Contemplative Psychology Program because I felt it paired well with my spiritual practice and my business practice working with clients. I was very lucky to get a very cool job running retail shops for a creative company. I was looking forward to the new adventure that was in front of me. Since the parasites in 2011 I had grown accustomed to a new way of living. I had stayed free of wheat and dairy and had kept off the weight I lost after during the candida and parasite detox. I was excited about my move to Boulder because I felt that Boulder would be a supportive environment for my health. Boulder, CO is well known for its 'granola' lifestyle. Most of the people that live there are very healthy and there are many grocery stores and restaurants that support people who are dealing with food allergies like wheat and dairy. I felt healthier just moving there! I was also looking forward to being in a new space to build new relationships. After analyzing my relationship with parasites; I had made major changes with my social scene. I was ready to connect with like-minded individuals who shared my same health and spiritual focus.

I remember my first week in Boulder. I had orientation at Naropa University and I also was opening a brand-new retail store. I had to meet my new team and set up the store as well as start to manage homework and a class schedule. This should have been an exciting time and normally I could handle all of that stress and ball juggling. Instead something was going on once again inside my body. My head swelled up, or was it my ears? I had chronic ear infections all my life, so I was familiar with the pain of an ear infection. But this was different. I felt like my equilibrium was off. I felt like my head was swollen and my ears were buzzing. I was really dizzy. My mom and sister had a history of ear problems and so I tried their remedies for equilibrium issues. They didn't work. The buzzing and dizziness stayed. It wasn't an inner ear issue. I had to go to work and school feeling out of sorts. I remember sitting at a family style restaurant in Boulder with my sister trying to eat something. I was really trying to take my mind off of my body's peculiar symptoms. A year and a half ago I had sat across from her in a similar restaurant. At the time I had just survived my night of steroid induced panic and sweats. I was so paranoid that day and here I was again; sitting across from her, hoping to release my fears. I couldn't stop talking about what was happening to me. I was looking to my sister for reassurance that I wasn't crazy or dying and that I would make it through this new set of bizarre physical symptoms.

Once again, I found my anxiety was triggered, and I started having panic attacks again. The illness back in 2011 had created a massive paranoia around health issues; especially around prolonged unexplained illness. I would walk into the office where I worked and have the shakes so bad from my anxiety I could barely hold myself together. I was trying to hide my symptoms because it was too confusing to explain to anyone. I made an appointment with my functional medicine doctor who had saved me back in 2011. I was hoping she would know just what to do for me. At my appointment I sat in the chair in the waiting room just writhing my hands. Being in her office was comforting and at the same time; it brought up all the fear I had the first time I had been there. In the appointment she said she didn't see signs of an ear infection and that she felt I needed to go back on the strict candida diet. I felt a bit defeated. I had stayed free of wheat and dairy but not of sugar. I ate a lot of gluten free options that still contained carbs and sugar. I thought overall, I was doing fine so I was confused what had triggered this sudden setback. I was also frustrated that my anxiety had become chronic again.

When I got home I found myself sitting on my couch and feeling panic welling up inside of me. I clung on to the pillow with my hands as tight as I could. I was holding on for dear life. I thought that perhaps I would lose my mind. I know I had changed everything and completely uprooted my life. Everything was different. Could this be triggering such major panic? Was I just not grounded? Sitting on my couch looking down at my hands. My fingers were raw from where I'd been biting them. There were scabs in some places on my thumb and forefinger where I'd ripped off the skin so much that I had bled. I thought to myself; *how long was I going to allow these behaviors to go on before I recognize that it is not 'normal' to function in this neurotic space?* This is not the first time I had suddenly become aware of an unhealthy behavior that had seemed normal to me for months, even years prior. The awareness of my neuroses was all too familiar. I had been looking in the mirror since I received Shaktipat back in 2008. In this moment I was fighting extreme anxiety. All of my life I have been a very 'type A' individual. My ability to function in high stress situations made me very good at the profession I had worked in for so many years. I could stay awake for hours to finish projects and often times had some of my most creative moments in the wee hours of the morning. My ability to multi-task and juggle many balls at once was part of my personality; or so I thought. What I hadn't 'seen' before this moment was that this was not typical behavior and was wreaking havoc on my system due to the high amounts of stress my body was expected to process. In my new awareness I had gained insight into this personality of mine; perhaps this was not my personality at all but instead a way I had subconsciously decided to cope with reality.

In coming to Boulder and specifically attending classes at Naropa; I was drawn to read a book called, Memories, Dreams, Reflections by Carl Jung. In that book he described his own neuroses. He explained that he was having fainting spells and had decided to overcome this. This was my first glimpse into analytical psychology. It was a great partner to the self-inquiry practice I already had. I decided I needed to take an analytical approach to my anxiety. I was overcome with panic attacks, anxiety and depression. Why was this? My mind had no ability to slow down. It was unable to stop and relax and suddenly I felt my mind clinging to anything it could. In this grasping for some kind of distraction from a state of rest I found myself tremoring with anxiety;

overcome with fear and unsure how to handle any of it. It seems so odd to me, that someone with so much training in meditation and contemplative practice was not able to slow down and work through the energy? I took advantage of a free write at the beginning of my creative class at Naropa to do some journaling about my anxiety. I found my notes from that class from August 30th, 2012.

Journal Entry

What the hell is up with this anxiety?? Anxiety what is it that you have to say to me that I'm not hearing? Too many changes all at once! You put yourself in an insecure position. You need to feel loved. What can I do to make myself feel secure and loved? Acknowledge myself.

An insight I had in asking these questions was; how long am I going to allow myself to move at the speed of light (even if that speed is an earthquake of sorts, shaking my body to the core with fear) before I decide to support myself? I had taught so many weight loss students the importance of supporting their immune system by not putting foods into it that cause it to over-process; in addition, supporting that same system with supplements they had become deficient in. Perhaps there was something my body needed that I was not giving it? I recognized in this moment that my body needed support. It did not feel secure in this new space and had absolutely no coping mechanism for actually slowing down. The first place I went was a deck of cards I love so much. The card I pulled was about Balance. I thought the Universe had quite a sense of humor as this was the very thing I was lacking. The message on the card was intriguing. It spoke of accepting things as they are. That there is no need for change and that there is only love. *I love and accept myself. I love and accept things the way they are.* Acceptance.

Over the course of the next few weeks I followed the candida diet with extreme discipline. I was determined to get my body and mind back into alignment. I had a bizarre instance in the shower where clumps of my hair fell out. This of course triggered another major panic attack. My doctor had put me back on antifungals and when I took them I felt so much brain fog from the immediate die off that I felt like I was going to float away. I was a complete mess! I had no idea how I had gone from feeling pretty energetic and stable over the past 18 months since the parasites to once again being completely off track.

Journal Entry 9-9-12

Here I sit by the creek side in my treasured mountains. I listen to the water run over the rocks; it bubbles and burbles. And the pine trees; I look up just now to see them and I see the moon above. What a precious place we live. How was ever such a thing made? I wonder. Finally coming out of my coma of sorts – a relapse in my health. I wonder – how do I stay in this place? It is here that I feel balanced and peaceful. I feel healthy and my creativity soars. Thoughts are expanded and words on paper flow effortlessly. I push myself too hard. I take on too much with no balance. If I spent each morning running or doing yoga, writing or sitting by this creek; would I have the energy to do all other things? Perhaps.

If I could keep my body clean…

What tempts me?

And have I forgiven myself? For pushing too hard, eating too much, not practicing safety and throwing caution to the wind?

I am willing to take risks – why am I willing to risk my Self?

A calm mind comes from trust and knowing there is always balance underneath the chaos.

I have to stop here to explain the deeper layers of this experience. I'm not sure how many of you have had an 'awakening' of consciousness. I'm certain as I speak of it; most of you will recollect one such experience. When one experiences a deeper awareness, there is an unfolding of energy. It's like suddenly the sun comes from behind the clouds and you see things in a clearer light. It's that moment when you suddenly see things differently or understand something in a way you did not before. For many of us, as we go through our spiritual awakening, this feeling can be powerful. And one layer will lead to another. The new awareness comes like the peeling back of a leaf on an artichoke. This leads to another leaf and another. You suddenly want to understand further or 'see' different experiences in your life that now validate your new-found awareness. Finally, you find yourself at the 'Heart' of the choke. Your own heart. You have integrated the new awareness and it has become a part of you. While it may come to the surface now and then for lessons or teaching; you will find that once a new insight is integrated; you no longer need to pull it up. It is simply part of you and you no longer question it or seek further answers.

For me, the first leaf was pulled away two years ago when I was first ill and trying to diagnose myself. Between periodontal infections, food allergies, parasites, supplements, acupuncture, energy work, chiropractors etc.; I stripped away each leaf on this artichoke. The heart came to me in that moment that I sat, two whole years later, staring at my half-bitten fingers.

We must support our own Selves.
There is no one else to do that for us.
It is not for us to place this responsibility on others.
If we can truly become utterly Present with
our Self; we will see the Truth.
This Truth is beyond a 'norm', a personality trait, or a psychosis.

It was in this moment that my new understanding made me realize something. In all of the change I had just put myself through; I had never come into acceptance of it. I also had never told my soul or my body that I was safe and that these choices were in fact going to support us for a healthier, happier life. I was actually completely disconnected from myself and because of this my pendulum had swung way off center. In that moment I saw the root of my anxiety and it ceased.

My own experience challenges us to look at our neurotic behaviors. The definition of neurosis is a class of functional mental disorders involving distress but neither delusions nor hallucinations, whereby behavior is not outside socially acceptable norms. This could be so many different things; from smoking to biting our nails, washing our hands before AND after every meal and so on. In fact, I am starting to think that most of our identities and/or personalities are based off of our neurosis. Let's take a first date for example. When we first sit with someone for a coffee or cocktail, we notice things about them. How they are dressed, how they order, even what they order and how they treat the Barista. After the initial body language, there is discussion. What do you do for work? Where do you like to eat? Divorced? Single? The questions go on. Each and every person has a 'story'. Their life story can be very different depending on who they are with, but there is one common link; our personality and our identity. "I am a teacher." "I am a banker." "I am gluten free." "I am a smoker." Underneath the identity are personality traits. "I am a workaholic." "I am a night owl." It's interesting to me that we claim these things as our own when they really have nothing to do with the essence of who we are. These identities or traits, or even quirks, are really how we are choosing to react to the outside world. They are our coping mechanisms that ground us in the world.

This takes me further into thinking that these traits are actually necessary in some way. If no one identified with anything; our world would be filled with lost souls. Or would it? What does it mean to disassociate yourself with the labels you have put on yourself? This is where the inner work comes in. In the teachings that I practice; it is not about letting go of who you are by forgetting about it or becoming no one. Instead, it is about looking at these labels, traits, personalities etc. and coming to understand them. What are they doing for you? How are they serving you? Each and every fragment of our selves is really a reflection of a lesson that we are learning. In looking at each fragment, we are able to discover more of our own Truth. This reveals the essence of our being and the root of its needs. Perhaps my own need to be the 'star' and to lead in every situation in my life is really my soul's need to be acknowledged. By acknowledging my own Self I discover the root of the personality trait and release it from the follicle.

I had my first experience with self-inquiry when I had first left my marriage. I was incredibly unstable after leaving my husband. I was incredibly lonely. Relationships I thought would work out hadn't. I was disappointed. I felt like I had failed as a psychic to stay balanced and had let my clients down. My finances were a mess and overall, I felt like I had taken 10 steps backwards…or maybe 100 steps. I was really trying to look at myself and what I had created for my life. I had just learned about the 'mirror'. This idea that we project all sorts of outward appearances and play all kinds of roles. These roles are reflected back unto us through our life experiences and the people we surround ourselves with. Essentially, we have mirrors all around us reflecting back what we need to see. This can be challenging. As a psychic I had 100's of clients who were mirrors. I would find myself giving them advice that I, myself, should have been taking! I often felt that I was living a lie because I would help so many and yet at the end of each day I was making the same mistakes. The reality was that the Universe was trying to show me what I needed to work on. I just need to be ready and willing to see myself – for real. I wrote about my many faces in my journal.

Journal Entry Fall 2009

I see a girl. She is smiling. She has ringlets in her hair. Her eyes sparkle like the blue in the sea. She is calling to me. She reaches out her hands asking mine to join hers; to become one. "Come and play with me!" She shouts. Oh, but my heart! My heart is crying. I feel a shattering deep within my soul. All that I was and all that I have known is blowing apart as though a bomb went off at the center of my knowing. I cling. Grasp to the pieces that are falling all around me. But as I pick up the pieces I see that they are all shards from the mirror. As I look into them I see my face; the many faces of my Self in the past. They stare back at me as though they know me and yet they are not me. They are not of me. They are not mine. They are pieces of myself as I was once known. When I see my Self; I see a girl. She has ringlets in her hair. She wears a Strawberry Shortcake dress with red shoes. She is a ballerina. She is a poet. She is a musician. She dances. She laughs. She is filled with joy. She is whole. She is one. She knows God. She carries the Shakti in her smile and in her laugh. Who are we really? Do we know that we are all just reflections of our own projections? When all the 'faces' die away; what is left? When we come to forget ourselves; do we remember God? When I see you; I see a mirror. Who do you want me to see? What image do you reflect? Is what you see when you look out the same as when others look in?

The reality is that none of us really 'see' each other for who we are. Think of the many conversations you have had with your friends. How many times did you share with someone what you thought about someone or something; only to have misinterpreted and repeated to others in a totally different light? Think of the many times you have 'felt' emotion for someone. We get caught up in what 'we' are feeling and begin to formulate opinions about what they must feel or think. By the time you have the conversation with that person or share what you feel; you begin to have the overwhelming sense that they are not at all in the same place as you; that they do not 'feel' for you that way or had not even given it a thought. These are examples of projections. Often times we 'project' our own emotions; our own 'consciousness' onto others. We do not 'see' what they are reflecting or what they truly feel within their own heart, within their own consciousness. We choose what we see. We decide what we will accept as reality and what is not. How many times have we heard the phrase, *no one understands me.* Many times, this is the case. What we don't realize is that we are misunderstood because we do not actually know ourselves.

When we are not familiar with the landscape of our own soul, then we are unable to 'project' the image of ourselves that we want others to see.

Instead, we project our fears, insecurities and emotions to the outside world. We project our 'egoic self'. Then we are not understood. No one sees you. Instead they see your ego, your identity. They see what has been created by the many voices inside your head. The teacher that told you that you couldn't sing; the father who told you that you were too fat. This is what is projected to the outside world. It isn't all negative. It can project the mother who told you that you could do anything you put your mind to; the old boyfriend who said you were beautiful. All of these images of yourself are each a piece of the mirror reflecting out into the world who you are.

What you must know is that this is, in actuality, not who you are. This is a 'reflection' of the mirror that has been created in your life. Who you are lies deep within the heart center. This is consciousness. The heart is where we are One with God. This is where we are perfect, beautiful; and contain only one emotion, love. When we are able to shatter the mirror and remove the many faces that were given to us by others; we can then come to know ourselves. We are then able to see and feel exactly who we are. We are able to experience the light of Truth, our own light. It is at this time that the projection dies away and all that is, is Self. The spirit of Self begins to shine forth to all others. You are understood. Others will 'see' you. What is reflected in their eyes is love, God and your soul. You will no longer feel pain. You will no longer be 'seen' as the emotions of the past that you were carrying. You will be seen as the soul that you are. You will be 'felt' as the essence of love that you feel.

This is but one step of the journey. One that all who wish to attain must take. It can be the most brutal and the most confusing. It is uncomfortable to learn that all that you knew of yourself and of others is not real but an illusion. Sometimes this can even be scary. It can feel as though there is no one you can trust and nothing to hold on to. It can also be the most challenging as you are squeezed into a space where you either cling to the past; which you know does not exist or let go and move into the great abyss of the void. There you will not find a branch to hold onto. There you float, in pure awareness. The energy of the past gone and there is no future to cling to. And we can learn this in a very brutal way. The most difficult experience to have is one where we are hurt, disappointed or let down by the 'reflections' being broken or revealed as their true identities.

When you look at me; who is it that you see?
Do you see my happy face, my smile, my all is well face?

119

*Or do you see my sad face, my nothing feels good
today face, my feel sorry for me face?
Do you see the singer, the poet, the creative story teller?
Or the writer, the thinker, the Hermit?*

The Shadow and Projections. Are they one in the same? Can 'projecting' our-selves be the same as our shadow? Are our projections really the shadow in disguise? I think so. Projecting happiness is just as unauthentic as projecting sadness or anger or any negative quality. And who are we projecting? It depends on who we are with. The roles I've played in my life are: The Psychic, the thinker, the philosopher…the happy, carefree I am happy with my choices girl can turn around and be the sad, lonely, I want to die girl. The singer, the writer and the dancer are all a role. So is the yogi, the meditator, the spiritual guru.

Being authentic is integrating all of these into one. Removing the bridge that separates them and bringing them together. How do we bring these dualities into one? By integration. How do we integrate all the roles that we play? By coming to terms with how each of these roles serves us and which roles are truly part of our authentic being. Becoming aware of when we are speaking our truth and when we are only telling a 'story'.

**Becoming aware of the different roles we play in our
lives enables us to 'see' ourselves with clarity.
This clarity brings a new-found awareness to our identities.
We become whole.
We recognize our patterns of behavior that are not authentic
or 'part of the whole' and we release them as baggage.
Integration happens.
Unity consciousness begins.**

Who am I? I am All. There is no I. I am a combination of all which means all roles, all dualities are me. I am one…we are one…one. ONE. There is no I or we, only one. Whatever I feel inside, inside my soul… is what is reflected outside. What you reflect is me. What I project is you. It is all the same.

The mirror can make or break a relationship. It can teach you the most important lessons of your life and help you to understand the deepest aspects of yourself. When you are building your circle of trust or are looking at the circle you presently have in place you will notice: The strongest relationships we have in our lives are with those mirrors that not only reflect the good; but the bad and the ugly. And those relationships can 'hold' the bad and the ugly without judgement or shame but instead with acceptance and grace. Having a support system to aid you in your journey of life is like having a pie crust able to hold even the gooiest of fillings. It is strong, it holds everything in while you continue to solidify and will still be there long after you have 'cut into' the deepest wounds of yourself.

My vision of 'cutting into it' is symbolic of when you become awake. When the new awareness arises, it is like that of cutting into a pie. The knife is thin and from one angle looks as though it is not even there. This small thin piece of metal has a power and strength to cut through the most difficult of substances. When cutting into a pie it suddenly reveals the filling. Just like a new awareness, the knife begins to release all that was 'held' within and you are changed. You cannot go back. You are not able to put yourself back together. You are open now. With openness comes vulnerability. Vulnerability raises so many emotional issues to the surface; fear, anxiety, worry and stress. But there is something about what bubbles up from underneath the crust; bitter and sweet, hopeful and enticing. You want to dig into it. And that is exactly what we are going to do. One of the seven Hermetic principles is the principle of polarity.

"Everything is dual; everything has poles; everything has its pair of opposites; like and unlike are the same; opposites are identical in nature, but different in degree; extremes meet, all truths are but half-truths; all paradoxes may be reconciled." The Kybalion

Where there is light; there must also be shadow.

In your new awareness, this shift in consciousness, a light begins to permeate the room that is your heart. In this room where you had never seen the walls; you now see the floor, the ceiling, the rocking chair that sits in the corner, the books that lay on the floor. With this new vision, the light now cast in your space; you also now see the shadows that dance on the walls. Those shadows call to you now; to dance with them. And so it shall be.

The Shadow

I sit and wait, no tears will come.
I shout and pound, yet no anger is undone.
I feel alone, afraid and weak.
Yet strong and brave, my path I seek.

At peace, I know my mind must feel.
Yet I cannot bow my head or kneel.
I dance around, singing songs of my past.
This shadow I feel, how long will it last?

In my head the thoughts race and race.
Not even I can keep up with the pace.
Not a moment of quiet in the day or night.
Nothing I do, seems to feel right.

All I want is to cry, to shed just one tear.
It seems months that I have been dealing with my fear.
When all is quiet, when all is at peace;
Will I allow myself that emotional release?

We have to learn to support ourselves. We are ultimately on this journey alone. There is no one else to understand you better than you. I think this is where the inner work can become tricky. Many of my friends and clients, including myself, are alone. Single folk are a breed of their own. Most of us are struggling with our loneliness, our fears and the extreme anxiety created knowing we have to 'go it alone'. We long for support, and we look for it. Unfortunately, what we find is that most are not up to the task. Even our close friends are not always able to handle the intensity of emotion and disarray that arises when dealing with loneliness and our individual neurosis. What to do? We have to find a way to generate support for both our system and our minds. We have to develop new coping mechanisms that are potentially healthier and more balanced than late night binges or desperate phone calls to our girlfriends. While those calls are sometimes necessary and can talk us off our emotional 'ledge'; they are also not the only answer. Co-dependency can support us in some way, but it is still (in my opinion) not the balanced way.

Moving to Boulder was the right decision for my health at the time. In hindsight it was more to support my overall journey of balance. It took about 30 days of the candida diet for the symptoms to start to dissipate. All the while I was having to push through work and my classes as though I was running at peak energy. What I learned during that time, and through the process of self-inquiry, was that I had never let go of all my distractions. By moving to a town that is somewhat isolated from the outside world I removed myself from familiar relationships and spaces. This created a great deal of anxiety because my ego wanted to cling to past distractions. I was starting over. That was really hard. Ironically, the discipline needed to follow the diet provided familiarity and routine where I had none. The introduction to psychology at Naropa was also changing me. I was starting to see the link between analysis of the mind and healing.

There is Suffering.

The first noble truth in Buddhism is that there is suffering. The first step in healing yourself is to become aware. To become aware is suffering. When your consciousness becomes awake; it realizes the existence of cyclical existence. In this realization; your mind experiences suffering. There is pain in the first moments you see yourself; just as there is pain in the first moments you are born into this world. Awareness is a re-birth. It is a single moment where your Soul comes alive in the world you have been sleepwalking through. The Light of Awareness brings you out of the dark and into the realm of consciousness.

Complete the following self-inquiry questions to examine your shadow and projections. Take all the time you need with the section.

Journal Entry

What tempts me?

Have I forgiven myself?

Have I risked my Self? Why?

List your labels, traits, personalities etc. What are they doing for you? How are they serving you?

What do you learn from this?

What image do you reflect? Is what you see when you look out the same as when others look in? Who are we projecting?

9

Releasing Your Karma

In addition to the energy systems of the body; there is also the concept of the karma and its effect on the human physical condition. I want to take this time now to explain how I feel about Karma and its effect on us as humans.

Krama is my own personal philosophy. It is a combination of 'drama' and 'karma'; which inevitably seem to go hand in hand. It seems that wherever we turn we have some sort of 'karmic' incident. And within that incident seems to be a great deal of drama. Whether the drama is emotional or physical; involves some sort of 'sign' or a relationship gone awry, the drama does exist. I want to first talk about Karma as I think many of us use this term without truly understanding its meaning. Prior to additional knowledge gained from study, I always thought of Karma as something that was 'meant to be'. It was something that happened because it was fated or because it was destiny. Karma, whether bad or good, was something that you could not control or eliminate and was part of your path or journey. If someone said, "That was Karmic."; most of us would think that they may have felt like they knew the person they had just met or that they felt that they didn't 'deserve' that accident but there was nothing to prevent it. Therefore, it must be 'Karmic'. I think that most of us misunderstand Karma as a reward or a punishment reaped from some other lifetime or experience. Most of us don't realize and do not take responsibility for the fact that we are still creating Karma. Yes, even at this very moment we are creating Karma. It isn't just that because we were a princess in another life and so therefore in this life we deserve to be a poor girl working at Pizza Hut and living on minimum wage. I know that you are laughing at this, but I also know that all of us have said something like this before. Karma is action. Any action. Any and all action is actually Karma. Good actions equal good Karma and bad actions or choices equal negative Karma.

Now, does past life Karma exist? Of course. Do we have soul mates? Yes…that is a whole other chapter. Can Karma bring two people together for better or for worse? Yes, and it has! If you fell in love with someone in another lifetime but never got to consummate the relationship; it may be Karmic for the two of you to be together in this lifetime. If you were with someone in a past life even though they were married; it could be Karma in this lifetime to lose this person to another. You may be drawn to someone you have never met because of Karma. You may be drawn to a job, a scent, a location or even a food because of Karma and past life experience. However, there is something that everyone must know. You do not have to experience Karma at its fullness. I will say this again.

You do NOT have to experience Karma at its fullness.

What does this mean? This means that just because you have Karma; it does not mean that you have to go through the entire experience surrounding this Karma. There are ways to clear and purify Karma without having the actual experience. One way is to have a guru or healer clear Karma for you. Now, my thoughts on this today is that can be an incredible experience and a gift. But…but, it can be equally fulfilling to learn how to work through your lessons by working on them yourself and therefore clearing or moving 'through' the experience much more quickly and with a lot less pain.

How do I clear my karma?

Simple. Eliminating Karma happens through a two-step process; identify the 'knots' of karma in your life and eliminate or 'smooth out' the knots. When you think of your life; think of what isn't 'working'. Perhaps you continuously have financial issues or maybe relationships don't work out or it could be as simple as a friend or a checklist that is always on your mind as though the project or the conversation wasn't 'finished'. To take this one step further, it could even be a physical issue; the knee that doesn't move properly or a constant back problem. All of these are examples of 'knots of karma'. They are areas of your life that for one reason or another are not working properly. Some of this could come from a past life or could have come from last week. It depends on the actions that you have taken to create this knot in the first place. Once you have identified the knot; it is time to straighten it out. Some karma can be cleared by simply recognizing it and releasing it. Other karmic knots can take months or even years to dissipate. It can take time to undo what you have ultimately created that is affecting your life in a negative way.

I'm going to give you an example on how to release and eliminate negative karma. Let's say that you have been having financial problems and they have continued for the last several years. No matter how you try; you can't get ahead and make ends meet and everywhere you turn there is some other bill or financial disaster. Clearly the situation is karmic...a past life issue could have created the initial problems but as they got worse and more debts were accrued you began creating more negative financial karma. Before you know it, you have so many knots of financial karma that you are unable to get ahead.

What do I do to clear my financial karma?

1. Look at the behaviors that you exhibited that created the financial blocks.

   That is correct. It was you who created this. Don't forget; we create everything. Begin by looking at what created this block in this lifetime by YOU. This is not the time to play the blame game. If you truly want to release the karmic knots you are experiencing; you have to be willing to look at yourself first.

2. Were these behaviors dharmic? What is Dharma?
   dhar·ma (där'mə, dûr'-)

n.

1. *Hinduism & Buddhism*
   a. The principle or law that orders the universe.
   b. Individual conduct in conformity with this principle.
   c. The essential function or nature of a thing.

2. *Buddhism*
   a. The body of teachings expounded by the Buddha.
   b. Knowledge of or duty to undertake conduct set forth by the Buddha as a way to enlightenment.
   c. One of the basic, minute elements from which all things are made.

Ultimately Dharma is 'right' conduct, speech, thought etc. It is the idea that all things have a universal order and balance. I believe this is true and that Dharma alone can provide countless teachings about balance in your life.

There are certainly more questions that will arise as you work through these questions and dig deeper into your financial patterns.

To release financial karma ask yourself the following self-inquiry questions.

Journal Entry

Have I been balanced with my finances at any point in my life?

Are the actions I have taken with my gains and towards my losses been in 'right action'?

What are my financial blocks teaching me?

What are they trying to tell me?

What have I learned from my financial mistakes? What am I learning now?

After completing the self-inquiry exercises above you are now ready to release your karma. It is quite a simple process. Thank your finances. Thank the blocks. Forgive yourself for the choices/decisions you made. Accept your situation and accept the responsibility you now have to bring it into balance. Depending on your situation it could take a week or the rest of your life to bring your financial state into balance. But, by learning the lessons and by holding yourself accountable for your decisions and choices; you are now releasing the knot of karma that you created.

It is important to note that the above activity and self-inquiry can be applied to any aspect of your life you would like to heal.

Awareness.
Wisdom.
Forgiveness.
Acceptance.
Right Action.
Karma cleared.

Awareness that Samsara, the wheel of Maya or illusion, exists brings deeper awareness to the Karma and Illusions you have created.

This deeper awareness leads to awareness of heavy energies, knots, toxins and blocks that are in your human life. This wisdom then leads to the desire to have a deeper understanding of your Self.

10

Mold

When I first met my doctor, she had a chart in her office. In the middle it said 'well'. Meaning feeling well. Below it was other words that meant ill essentially and at the top it said Vitality. I remember that vividly because it really struck me. I had thought I was fine being 'well'. After months of being ill and finding out there was illness and infection in every nook and cranny of my body; I wanted to be vital. I wanted to be free of all disease and be happy and healthy - really healthy. Since that moment I did in fact get healthy and stay relatively so. I was completely dairy and wheat free which made a huge impact on how I felt. I kept the weight off that I lost when I was on the candida diet to kill parasites and had come fully back into balance after my strange 'attack' in Boulder. I had also gotten into really great shape at the gym with the help of a personal trainer and ran my first set of marathons. It is amazing how subtle the steps are to reach your goals. I had always wanted to have clearly defined muscles but could never even get that far because my weight and energy was such a struggle. With my new diet I had eliminated the heavy weight burden and my energy had peaked and I was able to achieve my goals.

In 2016 I had been parasite free for 5 years. After the parasites and food allergies were revealed to me I stopped taking so much for granted. I put my health at a much higher priority. I made sure I ate whole foods when I could and found the brands and local places that were safe for me to eat. I always remembered the time I nearly died and joked about it with most people. In my heart it was no joke. I remembered all the panic and fear that I had and how challenging it was to be completely alone for most of the time I was dealing with it. I didn't say no to anything anymore. I traveled even if I was alone and I jumped into things that felt right without thinking twice. I had met the Dalai Lama during that time and I lived on Maui for just under a year as well. I was living life and grooving off of all the positive changes I had made. But the thing about autoimmune disease is that you really don't know when it might rear its ugly head. I didn't know it at the time, but I really had only gotten the first layer of the story of my health when I found out about my food allergies and the parasites. In March of 2016 I began yet another life changing journey with great thanks to my poor health.

I went to Maui to visit friends. I was only there for about 5 days and had a really great time. When I returned I felt pretty fatigued? But I know my system and at the time chalked it up to all the travel. I had gone to San Francisco to a fashion exhibit the month before and was planning on going to Phoenix to visit my dad in another month as well. I was very busy. The store I was managing was closing and I was taking advantage of the last of my commission and bonuses to go on some trips. A couple of days after getting back from Maui I had dinner. Following dinner, I had a bizarre episode. My throat seemed to swell up and panic ensued. I do believe I have PTSD to this day from my first bout with bizarre illness. Any symptom that is odd triggers full on panic for me. Anyways, my throat seemed to swell, and I had a hard time breathing. I took Benadryl thinking it was an allergy attack, but it didn't feel that way and the Benadryl did nothing. I got in my car thinking I would go to urgent care. Then I remembered all the times I went to urgent care and they did nothing when parasites were eating my body. I went anyways. And they sent me home. I still regret going that night. I told myself that I was just overreacting because of everything I went through in 2011 and that it was nothing and I needed to calm down and go to sleep. I seemed fine the next day.

To give some back story here; ever since I had lived on Maui I had started experiencing some strange health issues. My sinuses seemed to swell up for no reason and I had gained some weight back. Not much but it was enough I noticed. I had irregular heartbeats and sweating, and my hormones were out of whack. I even had an episode just a few days after arriving back in Colorado where my heart started beating so fast I nearly fainted. I was dizzy and sweating and even putting my head between my legs did nothing. It was scary, but I thought it was just a fluke with so much change going on due to the move. None of this was enough to draw my attention. It was subtle, and nothing compared to what I had dealt with in previous years. And so much had healed because of my diet and lifestyle changes. I didn't put much stock into it. My doctor was great but very expensive. Insurance doesn't cover Functional medicine of course. I didn't want to bother with an appointment if nothing serious was going on. Well those are famous last words. Another piece worth noting is that when I got to San Francisco off the plane I felt extremely fatigued and dizzy. The hotel didn't seem to help either. I ended up walking outside to get my bearings. A few weeks after the supposed allergy attack I got a kitty. I had not gotten a pet since my Max died in 2008. I have to share about Max's death because it is my first real experience managing through death. Losing Max began my journey of understanding death and starting to come to understand it.

With life; there is also death.

Max

My little piggy. Max was my Basset Hound. He was my dog for 7 years. I adopted him when he was 2 years old. He smelled, and his toenails were always way too long. His ears always got dirty and he had many accidents in the house. Yet, he was my baby and I loved him very much. Max and I had a wonderful telepathic connection. I was able to read his thoughts and he could read mine. He was a healer. He took on a lot of negative energy from those who spent time with him. He was always making sure everyone was happy. Seeing him wag his tail and smile the way he did was enough to brighten anyone's day. Max had a lot of issues with his body. He even had to have his stomach stitched up after cutting himself on a hanger. I know he didn't like his body much. He hated being low to the ground and the many physical limitations that came along with it. But somehow, he managed to hike with me in the mountains, run and play with other dogs and still have a wonderful quality of life.

One day I was meditating and decided that I wanted to have a vision. Sounds silly I am sure. When one is developing their psychic abilities, you get to a point where I think you just want something to happen to prove you are really doing something. My advice; watch what you ask for. I did have a vision that day. I became completely overwhelmed by sadness and a 'knowing' that Max was going to pass away. I told my now ex-husband what I saw that afternoon. He thought I was crazy and part of me did too. Max was only 9 years old and although he was losing sight in one eye and had gotten gray I couldn't imagine him ailing. Although I wasn't sure what to think I spent the next month letting him sleep on my bed and paying extra attention to him. I'm glad I did.

August was right around the corner and you could feel that summer was slowly slipping away. I had just gotten home from running errands for a couple hours. The dogs greeted me at the door. Always enthused when one of us came home. I looked down at Max and saw that his entire neck was swollen. I immediately put my hands on him and felt these hard masses where his lymph nodes are. They were not there that morning and I just couldn't believe how suddenly he had swollen. I assumed that he must have gotten bitten by some kind of bug and was having an allergic reaction. I got him into the car and drove immediately to our local vet. As I was driving there I noticed Max. He loved to ride in the front seat. He would sit with his big barrel chest puffed out and his head out the window. Today he had this look; it was happiness and a sense of peace.

I suddenly realized what was happening. I said to him, 'you cannot leave me now…it isn't time…don't go from your mama…'. What I had realized is that he knew it was his time. He was ready to leave the body that had been so uncomfortable for him and go on to better things. By the time I got to the vet I was crying because I feared the worst. They got him in right away and when I was called into his room I knew it couldn't be good. He was diagnosed with Lymphoma. They said that we could try to save him and that if we did nothing he would pass within days. I was devastated. My premonition had come to pass. I left the veterinary clinic devastated. I was so sad to think that my little boy was going to leave me. I had opted out of the treatment. I knew from Max's energy and behavior that he didn't want to go through all of that. As I drove home with him next to me he was smiling and looking out the window. He truly did embody the qualities of a master. There was no fear, no worry, no fatigue. Even with his neck swollen and his life fading.

They gave him only 7 days.

The seventh day came. He had practically stopped eating. In pain, he couldn't walk. He mainly slept on his bed or with me on mine. His love of 'people food' wasn't even surpassing his lack of appetite. He was tired. It was late in the evening; probably around ten o'clock. As I got ready for bed I noticed Max limping to his bed. He was shaking. I took some blankets and put them around him and just held him. That night I prayed and prayed. I couldn't sleep. I slept with Max on the floor of my bedroom and held him while he shook. I was certain he was going to leave. I asked the angels;

Please. Please, give him whatever he wants. He has been such a good boy. He deserves to have whatever it is that he wants.

I awoke the next morning on the floor next to my boy. He was awake. He was wagging his tail. He was alive! The swelling was completely gone. He went downstairs and ate his breakfast. I was in shock. So was my husband! For the next 2 weeks Max played like he hadn't played in years. He played with his brother Caesar and with our kitty. All of our family came to visit during this time, auspiciously, and he got to see them all. He ate and barked and howled. It was an incredible gift that the Angels had given him and us. At the end of the two weeks my husband awoke me to tell me that Max had gone outside to go potty and just laid down in the grass. I went outside. Max laid there with difficulty breathing. The swelling had returned. There was no moon. The 4am sky was black and full of stars. I laid down next to Max on the dewy grass and looked up at the stars. We talked. I told him how much I loved him and just took in that moment; there in the grass with the stars above.

We put him to sleep at 5pm that day. The angels came and took his soul before they had even finished the injection. My mother got a puppy a few months later who was born on the same day that Max passed.

The cycle of Birth, Death and Re-birth.
Samsara.
Consciousness brings you 'out' of the cycle.
Having become awake; you realize Truth.
Truth is what sets you free.
Freedom is Liberation.

I had been wanting a dog for many years since Max had passed but the kitty needed a home and I thought it was time. I loved her right away. She slept with me every night. She was so sweet, and we bonded immediately. At the same time however, I noticed that I was getting some bad allergies and sinus issues. I didn't think it was the kitty since I had cats most of my life and they never bothered me. I did have trees blooming outside my window and figured that was why my eyes were crusty when I woke up in the morning.

Now this next part is the weirdest. I was leaving work like I did every day and I grabbed the office door and I could barely move it! I am pretty strong. Even with all my health issues I was a cheerleader and had gotten my shape back and could most certainly lift a door! But I couldn't. It was far too heavy. And I didn't feel well. I thought maybe I was getting a cold. Nothing that a little sun couldn't cure. I was looking forward to my trip to Phoenix to visit my dad. I was only gone three days, so I left the kitty at home and went on my trip. At my dad's house

I had a really hard time. I was extremely exhausted after we were in the sun all day. More exhausted than what would be considered normal. I also still had crusty eyes and sinus issues. On top of that I was feeling pretty pudgy compared to my normal self. I remembered the channels telling me years ago, when I was battling candida, that I would become bloated and pudgy when I was out of balance with my health. I shook that thought off. I felt like I probably needed to go back on the candida diet again and it would solve the weight problem. It was only a 2-day visit in Phoenix and I found myself back at home and feeling pretty run down. Again, I thought it was just travel and allergies and went to bed.

The next day was Memorial Day. I had signed up to run the Bolder Boulder. I had done it the two previous years and it was a challenge to do this 10k run. I got up and went to the race even though I was feeling off track. I got there and got in line. I felt really hot and I almost left and went back to my car. I knew I wasn't up to it. But I went ahead and ran it. Unlike previous years I had to start walking clear into mile 1. I also was so fatigued and so dehydrated. I had terrible cotton mouth and felt like my legs were Jell-O. I did finish the whole thing even though I walked most all of it. When I sat down at the end of the race I could barely feel my legs. It was awful. I went home and went to bed. The next morning, I couldn't feel my legs. Literally. When I pushed down on the skin I could not feel my fingers. It was like they were numb. But when I went to lift them up I could move them, so I knew I wasn't paralyzed. The other scary thing was that my arms and legs were extremely heavy. I could barely move them! Something was terribly wrong. The first thing I thought was here we go again with some weird health stuff and I have no idea what to do.

I kind of feel like the next week was a bit of a whirlwind. I tried to go to work but couldn't. I seemed to be getting worse. I didn't recover from the race and instead my arms and legs got worse. I still couldn't feel them, and they were heavier. I also started having panic attacks again. This time I had strange neurological issues that set off the panic attacks. I would have tweaking again, or I would feel my body quiver like electricity was going through it. The worst part was that when I got in the shower in hot water my right hand curled up and my body twitched. It was literally the scariest thing that I have ever experienced in my life and I see dead people!

Luckily this time I had a great doctor who specializes in weird autoimmune issues and saved my life back in 2011. I was able to get on her working list and luckily; they could get me in that very next week. That was a long week. I started to have respiratory symptoms. I couldn't breathe, and it felt like I had asthma even though that was never anything I had. My breathing was very heavy and shallow. My legs and arms were still incredibly heavy, and my legs were numb to the touch. I spent hours lying in bed just lifting my legs and arms up and down and touching them to see if I was going to be paralyzed. I couldn't take showers or baths without the water being cold. Hot water made my right arm curl up so bad I was too freaked out to deal with it. My weight changed drastically. I lost 20 pounds in two weeks. It made no sense. My hair also started to fall out in huge clumps. It dawned on me that this hair loss was exactly what happened back in Boulder a few years earlier.

Now I've been through this before; the strange illness that no one can diagnose. It is enough to make you lose your mind. You can't think straight. You are always in a panic. Your anxiety is so high that your adrenaline is constantly rushing, and you aren't sure what will happen next. This was not at all like I had experienced before. It was very different. The neurological issues were the scariest. Did I suddenly have MS? Was something wrong in my brain? I couldn't breathe, and I couldn't move my legs. I couldn't even bathe. I was so defeated. All this time of maintaining good health after the last incident and here I was again fighting through something that made no sense. What happened? I just couldn't figure it out. But much like the first time I was determined to find the answer to my problem. My Tarot cards looked as bleak as they did in 2011. This illness was going to be here awhile, and I knew all I could do was fight through it.

My doctor had requested an MRI because of my symptoms. She sent me in for it before I went to my appointment. I appreciated that my doctor always wanted data to understand what was happening with my health. I had learned a lot about my health and how my body functioned because of the data she had gathered over the years and subsequently explained. She also sent me to an Otolaryngologist who also practiced Integrative medicine.

Find the teachers, doctors and healers that you trust that can help you to begin your journey. Find out as much information as you can about your body and yourself.

She knew that my issue may have to do with allergies because of the respiratory issues and she wanted my ears checked because of the heaviness I was feeling and the vision issues. I went to the Otolaryngologist. He was very kind and told me he felt like my eye, nose and respiratory issue had to be from allergies and sent me home with petri dishes to put around the house. There is always some bizarre test you have to do. When I had parasites; I had to scrape my own feces into what looked like a French fry container and seal it in baggies. Now I was scraping dust and whatever else was lurking in my apartment into petri dishes to be sent to a lab.

The MRI was scary. I was so messed up physically and emotionally and on top of that I am pretty claustrophobic. My sister went with me. I was really scared that I had something wrong with my brain that was causing my body to go numb and my hand to curl up. My sister was very supportive and kept me in good spirits while we waited. I went in to the room and just took a deep breath. I knew I had to be brave enough to handle what they may see. An MRI is kind of strange. You lay down and go inside a little tube and there are all these very loud noises. You are trying to be calm and yet my entire life was being completely torn apart. It was only a short time ago that I was traveling and dating and having fun.

I want to address the social aspect of illness here. I mentioned my social anxiety that seemed to peak during my previous bouts of illness. Each time I couldn't even touch my phone. I didn't do much with that in 2011 but I noticed this pattern and decided to take a look at it this time. When we are sick with a disease; especially with these bizarre autoimmune diseases, you become extremely sensitive to everything. I could literally feel the electricity coming out of the phone and did not want it to touch me. I was exhausted just thinking about some of my relationships and no longer wanted to maintain them. The first time I was ill it actually disintegrated a few of my closest relationships. This second time around it did much of the same. Not just my platonic relationships but my dating relationships too. It suddenly becomes clear who matters. The number one person who matters is you. Your boundaries become clear. It is a lovely blessing inside of an illness. The disease actually shows you where else in your life you are experiencing dis-ease but just weren't paying attention to it because you were busy distracting yourself.

It was finally my appointment day with my doctor. I was so looking forward to seeing her. I had cried for the past several days. I was scared and alone and tired. I remember walking into her office and I felt like death warmed over. I was a mess. My hair was so thin, and I could barely walk. I was anxious for my test results and wondered what she was going to say to me. My doctor has a warmth about her. She is kind and gentle and even when she gives you tough news you just feel like everything is going to be okay. She had me sit down and began to go over the results of my MRI. Mold was the issue. She said that she is certain I have a genetic mutation that causes me to be highly affected by mold. She mentioned CIRS; Chronic Inflammatory Response Syndrome[27]. CIRS is defined on Dr. Shoemaker's website as "An acute and chronic, systemic inflammatory response syndrome acquired following exposure to the interior environment of a water-damaged building with resident toxigenic organisms, including, but not limited to fungi, bacteria, actinomycetes and mycobacteria as well as

---

[27] For more information on CIRS http://www.survivingmold.com/news/2014/12/what-is-cirs/

inflammagens such as endotoxins, beta glucans, hemolysins, proteinases, mannans and possibly spirocyclic drimanes; as well as volatile organic compounds (VOCs)." She also said that I had a small white colored mark on my MRI that I needed to talk to a specialist about. There were many blood tests ordered and a ton of supplements I went home with. I felt like I was getting closer to my diagnosis, but I felt very far away from being well. I was once again on the candida diet and this time there were new mold rules. I knew what it was going to take to get well and that I may go a few weeks before I really knew the full diagnosis. Just like the last time I was sick there were going to be more tests before I had answers. It was going to take strength and perseverance to make my way to the other side. I had a card from The Tao Oracle[28] card deck on my altar. This card was Discipline. I placed it on my altar back in 2011 when I first had to follow a strict detox diet.

"When the time to mobilize 'the army' has arisen, it is a clarion call for self-discipline and much needed clarity that is tripped of emotional excess and undaunted by mounting chaos. It may seem now that you are surrounded on all sides by potentially undermining forces that threaten to chip away at the foundation you stand for. This is neither the time to act hastily nor the time to allow the present conditions to continue any longer without your intervention in the hope that they will change of their own accord." The Tao Oracle

The blood tests were intense. Always a lot of vials of blood taken out of your body when they are testing for autoimmune issues. It's the worst. I fainted of course. I was so weak in all areas that I don't think I could have stayed conscious if I wanted to. I remember going back home to my apartment after those tests and just laying down on my bed. My whole body was numb. I couldn't cry anymore, and I couldn't take care of myself either. I really felt like maybe this time I was done here. I was totally alone. Friends had abandoned me and so had the man I had been dating. Even some of my family just didn't know what to do

---

[28] The Tao Oracle https://www.amazon.com/Tao-Oracle-Illuminated-Approach-Ching/dp/0312269986

for me. I was grateful for my sister and a few friends who came and washed my sheets and got me some groceries, so I could eat. It was just awful. I am very independent and at the time I really loved my solitary space. It was hard to ask for help and hard to be alone at the same time. One of my friends sat with me when I first started taking antifungals again. I remember that same floaty feeling I felt in Boulder. I could barely stay focused to form a sentence. The brain fog was completely overtaking me.

It had been a week since I sent in the Petri dishes and a few days since I saw my doctor. I felt unsafe in my home. I felt like something was silently lurking that was slowly killing me. My breathing was so bad now that you could hear my raspy breathing out loud in my apartment. Unable to really walk I tried to pull myself up to make some food. As I made one of my staple candida diet dinners my previous sickness came flooding back to me; the chanting and the fear, the diligence I had to have to stay on track. How did this happen again? Why?

That night I lay in my bed. I felt a darkness come over me like I had never felt before. I was ready to give up, but I was so scared of dying. I thought about the Dalai Lama. He was actually coming that summer. I was one of the volunteer coordinators and had fallen a bit off track with this illness. I wondered; what would he say? I thought he would probably laugh his amazing laugh and tell me that everyone dies and that it is, in fact, a part of life. I remembered the Osho Zen Tarot and how Osho talks about how we all come into the world alone and we leave this world alone as well. I laid in a heap on my bed unable to move or feel my body and I thought I just can't be scared. I felt the presence of death all around me. I took a deep breath and I realized I have to look at this even if I am afraid. What if I die? What if I die right now tonight? I closed my eyes and imagined just letting go. I felt my fear turn from a tight knot in my stomach and an intense holding on to an ease and a relief and I opened my eyes. I looked at the pictures of Paris hanging on my bedroom walls. They were all pictures I took when I was there with my mom 3 years earlier. I looked at my bust form that all of my necklaces hung on. I took that bust form after a store remodel a few years ago and I just loved it. It reminded me every day how much I loved fashion. I looked at my mala hanging on my altar. The mala was given to me by a dear Tibetan woman that I met in Washington D.C. I had worked as a volunteer for the Kalachakra shortly after I got well from the last bout of illness. That was a special time as I got to meet the Dalai Lama on the last day I worked there. I remembered that time.

Journal Entry

I awoke out of a sound sleep to my phone going off. I grabbed it in a panic as it was my new friend Max. I was hoping it was the call I had been waiting for. "He's allowed an audience!" she shouted. "Be there by 6:15!" I bolted out of bed. It was so early, and the room was pitch black. My roommate awoke and asked if it was the call and I assured her it was. I hurried and put on the same clothes I had worn for two full weeks. Today was day 12 and I could not believe it was really the end. Once outside the hotel, the morning light was faint and soft. The sun was not yet out but the sky was beginning to fade from purple and pink to the soft blue of the morning sky. The street lights were still shining. It was early morning, the time of night when you feel like you should just be returning home from the bar. Too early to be out running and too late to still be in party mode.

In my rush to get to the Verizon Center I hailed a cab. I had not realized that the subway did not run so early in the morning on Sunday. I could only hope the cab would show up and get me there on time. He arrived quickly and assured me he could reach Chinatown in time. As I sat in the cab, half-panicked and half-excited, I noticed my body. My legs were sore and even my buttocks from working the booth all day every day. I had put in 12–15-hour days each day I had been here. Hardly any rest from having to wake so early to take the subway in; I was exhausted and swollen. Finally, we arrived at the center and I ran in to the Volunteer lounge.

"Line up here!" shouted the volunteer coordinator. We waited rather impatiently as they led us into a separate space in the basement of the Verizon center where risers had been set up. They placed us all on the risers. All of us donning our blue Volunteer shirts and waiting anxiously to see Him. Secret

service came into the room and stood in front of us. "Do not touch Him in any way or you will end up on the ground with one of us on top of you!" Although they were joking, we also knew they really were not.

As if by magic, suddenly there he was. The entire room filled with light. It was as though a bubble of clear liquid light had blown from his very heart and the fragments scattered all through the room. You could feel this pure clear light penetrate your skin, your cells and go deep into your DNA. Suddenly my heart was expanded, open and in a state of existence I had never known before. And His presence, it was so great, so large. From the stage he seemed so small, a simple Buddhist monk as he always put it. Here, in person he was tall, strong and I suddenly felt safe. Vulnerability melted into nothingness. Then he came towards me. He looked into my eyes as he stood right before me, acknowledging my presence. He turned as it was time for the picture. I am not certain even now how the picture came with my eyes facing forwards. I was mesmerized by my Guru, here before me. Years of meditation and practice with teachings coming only in whispers during the silence or through a random internet post. He had a thousand ways to reach me every single day and yet I did not think I could reach him. And yet here I stood with my heart pressed against his robes. I could feel his strength and in my mind, I could hear him tell me, 'see I am always near,' and laugh his infectious laugh that no one can imitate. It ended as quickly as it began. He was soon no longer in the room and we were off to our booths and to help setup for this last grand day. I have never received a greater gift.

Looking at everything around me I thought; it is okay if I go now. I have been all over and have seen so much. I thought of the romances I had and the gift of healing I received from living on Maui. I had done all sorts of things I had never expected, and I knew how lucky I was. I had a good life. In that moment this overwhelming feeling of hope poured over me. I heard a voice that said; what if you live? In that moment I contemplated that question. If I lived I would live differently. I would stop being afraid. I would find my true companion and I would have a family. I would help as many people as I could and try to live up to the Bodhisattva vows I had taken back in 2009. It was such an empowering moment. I felt I had overcome death and that nothing could stop me from healing.

I woke up the next morning and everything felt different. It is difficult to explain but when I opened my eyes and looked around my room it was as though I was looking at someone else's room. I looked at those same Paris pictures and it was like I was looking at someone else's life and was just visiting their room. It was so strange. I got up and still felt terrible, but I knew I had made it through the tunnel of death and was now standing on the other side. As I made it to the kitchen I got a phone call from my ENT. He said that my lab results came back and that my kitty had black mold on it! What? They had me swab that kitty and sure enough it was killing me! I had to give the kitty up immediately. I couldn't believe it. I knew that I had to make arrangements for the kitty right away so that I could begin the process of getting well. It was tough to take the kitty to a new owner. I hadn't had a pet in so long and just loved her being with me. Unfortunately, her sleeping with me every night was what was causing these symptoms to escalate. After the kitty had been taken to someone who could clean her and take care of her I had a dear friend come clean my apartment. We washed EVERYTHING! I had to make sure all of the remnants of black mold were gone from my home.

I got lucky. I got lucky because this was just mold on a cat. There are thousands of people who are dealing with mold in their homes. There are even people sleeping in tents in their backyard because they can't sleep in their home because it is killing them. For weeks after this incident I was still panic stricken that something else was in my apartment making me sick. I even made arrangements to transfer to a new complex across town so that I was out of the area I was living in. I cannot really explain the paranoia that comes with dealing with mold. If you are there, then you understand. You feel like the unseen is attacking you and at any moment you can walk into a place that is going to make you sick. Even now, two years later, I still can walk into an old building or a musty space and know that it has mold and I immediately feel dizzy and know I need to leave.

It was about 2 days after I found out that the cat had black mold that I found myself back in my doctor's office. She had gotten my results from the blood tests. I had the genetic mutation that causes the mold sensitivity as she had suspected. I also had CIRS. In addition, I flagged for Lyme's Disease, Epstein Barr Virus, Pneumonia and various other autoimmune issues. Just like in 2011 I had zero B12 in my system and was also flagging for high levels of inflammation. I had to not only stay on the candida diet, but I had to adjust for mold and that included taking Cholestyramine which is a binder to pull toxins out of your body. It is a horrible powder that I had to take 4 times a day on an empty stomach to pull the mycotoxins out of my body. My doctor prepared me that this was going to be a tough road. She explained that the binder re-exposes the toxins to my body and I will get sicker before I get better. She told me to stay strong. One thing I appreciate about my doctor is that she tells you the honest truth about what to expect and that makes me totally trust her when she tells me the outcome will be good. It gave me the strength to persevere.

I left her office and went to pick up the rest of the items I needed to get well. It was expensive. This is another challenge with mold. Insurance covers none of it. And it is extremely costly. Between the whole foods you have to buy and the supplements and the binders it cost over $10,000 for me to get well. This included me being unable to work for 3 months while I focused on getting well. You lose your sense of security in your home and you also can lose your job. It's an awful thing to go through. I reiterate THOUSANDS of people are suffering from this problem and I think thousands more don't even know this is the issue. What I learned from my doctor is that so many weight issues, autoimmune issues and chronic illness are caused by mold and CIRS. It's crazy to think that this could all be healed through diet and proper methylation.

I want to explain further my diagnosis. I have the MTHFR genetic mutation. Both genes are actually mutated which means I am double heterozygous. This means that my body does not methylate or detox properly. The toxins over my lifetime have actually been building up in my body. At the time I was 37 years old which means I had 37 years of toxins accruing in my system. It was causing me to be susceptible to illness. It was why I had acne at 37 years of age. I had always had what they call cystic acne which are hard pimples that form and take weeks to go away. That is a sign that you have this issue. It was why I was having hormone issues and weight issues. It was also why I likely got 3 different parasites that nearly killed me back in 2011. My body could not eliminate them like a 'normal' person would because my body isn't able to. I also had CIRS or Chronic Inflammatory Response Syndrome. This meant that my immune system overreacts to any toxin that comes in contact with it. When I come in contact with mold my sinuses immediately swell up when someone else may not notice it at all. I also had several autoimmune diseases or viruses sitting in my body that can reappear at any time. They lay dormant just waiting for me to become susceptible and then they reappear. In addition to all of this I had the food allergies I discovered years before.

This all sounds overwhelming but really it just means that I am sensitive. That may sound like I am putting it lightly and maybe it is but that is how I look at it. In order to keep my immune system strong and to ensure that these illnesses do not reappear; I have to eat to live and to support my system. I have to stay on binders to keep my system free of toxins and I have to take extra vitamins to support my system because it does not keep a sufficient number of vitamins on its own.

The mold detox was awful. The first few days I took the CSM (Cholestyramine) I had immediate reactions. I had the throat swelling sensations that I had a few months prior. That feeling like you are having an allergic reaction, but you are really just reacting to the mold. My breathing was rough, and I still couldn't take a hot shower. My hair was still falling out. I would sit and look at the scalp showing through on the top of my head and just cry. I was still panicked that I would never come all the way back from this. The CSM also pulls the hormones out that help manage your thyroid. My thyroid actually got so bad that my voice became hoarse and scratchy. I sounded like I'd been a smoker for 20 years even though I never smoked. I had bouts of extremely low energy because of the thyroid issues as well. I was diagnosed with Hashimoto's. Sometimes I was hypothyroid and sometimes I was hyperthyroid. Because I was practiced in mindfulness from the last illness and a decade of spiritual work I was aware of all the subtle shifts in my body. I am thankful for that because in many ways it saved me. I became aware of when I was hypothyroid and was able to manage it with supplements like L-Carnitine. I remember that when I would take it my voice would suddenly go back to normal and I thought; oh, here I am! Then it would flex back. Sometimes I took too much and was suddenly hyperthyroid and was starving and anxious and then my energy would crash. I spent weeks, literally weeks, adjusting and re-adjusting the L-Carnitine to balance my thyroid. I had to continue the CSM to remove the toxins and as long as I was on that I had to try and save my thyroid. My doctor told me it was likely the CSM would burn my thyroid out and I may always struggle with Hashimoto's. That was hard to hear and so I just kept working on it in hopes that I would salvage it. I used Endoflex[29], an essential oil for the Endocrine system, and practiced yoga postures to try and support my thyroid and adrenal glands.

While you are taking CSM you have to also do a vision test online to check for mold in your body. It was interesting because I had far more mold in my right eye than my left. That right eye had always been weaker, and my glasses prescription was always treating that eye for astigmatism. I had a big aha moment doing this test because I realized the blurry vision was likely not astigmatism but instead mycotoxins. If you want to take the vision test go to http://www.survivingmold.com/store1/online-screening-test. You are directed to take it every 30 days when you are taking binders. I admit that I took it every 2 weeks. It was actually really motivating to watch it get better and better. I set a goal for myself that once it was green for both eyes that I would go off the CSM and switch to Charcoal.

After two weeks of taking CSM and following the candida diet I knew so well at this point; I started to feel much better. The energy had

---

[29] Endoflex is an essential oil from Young Living Oils https://www.youngliving.com/en_US

come back into my arms and legs. I still was having neurological issues. I thought that would never go away! But the heaviness was starting to leave my body. This reminds me of a reading I got during the worst of the illness. Prior to my doctor visit I made an appointment to have a skype call with my most trustworthy teacher from the Bahamas. At this point she had now been working with me since I was married and just beginning my journey as a psychic. I trusted her vision and her Siddha Yoga practice more than any other healer and psychic I knew. I am reminded now of talking to her about how I felt. I felt that the Universe was literally pinning me down, so I could not move and had to stop all my distractions and focus on myself. I remember telling her that I wondered if I would ever walk again. She told me I would heal and that she saw me hiking mountains again. That was such a relief. And as my energy was coming back I held on to the fact that I would get well again.

One big difference between my last major illness and this one is that I had a much stronger ability to be in my process. I was very blessed that both of these illnesses, even though they both took me to the edge of death, were quickly overcome. Quickly meaning a matter of months. I know that others have struggled with CIRS, mold, candida or other autoimmune diseases for years so to recover in just a few months was an incredible gift. I know that my discipline and my willingness to face it head on were part of the swift transformation. I am a Scorpio and because of that am willing to face the shadow. It is why awareness is so important.

There were two books I was led to read during this intense time. The first was *The Tibetan Book of Living and Dying*[30] and the second was *Waking the Tiger*[31]. After that night where I felt I had faced death head

---

[30] The Tibetan Book of Living and Dying by Sogyal Rinpoche https://www.amazon.com/Tibetan-Book-Living-Dying-International-ebook/dp/B000FC147G/ref=sr_1_1?ie=UTF8&qid=1524162766&sr=8-1&keywords=the+tibetan+book+of+living+and+dying+sogyal+rinpoche

[31] Waking the Tiger: Healing Trauma by Peter Levine https://www.amazon.com/Waking-Tiger-Healing-Peter-Levine-ebook/dp/B002IYE5XO/ref=sr_1_1

on; I decided to read The Tibetan Book of Living and Dying. I owned the book but had never read it. I pulled it off my bookshelf because I thought it might help me understand the teachings behind death. This book is quite profound, and I highly recommend it if you are facing the idea of death. As humans, we are scared of death. This book talks about how you must face those fears. We cannot escape death and we have to go through it alone. This book brought a strange kind of peaceful acceptance of death for me.

"There is no place on earth where death cannot find us – even if we constantly twist our heads about in all directions as in a dubious and suspect land…If there were any way of sheltering from death's blows – I am not the man to recoil from it…But it is madness to think that you can succeed…" Montaigne

Waking the Tiger was also a profound book for me and my long-term struggle with anxiety. The general concept of the book is that our anxiety is our animal 'fight or flight' instinct that is buried deep within us. We are no longer running from wild animals, but our anxiety and panic thinks we are. There was a process described in the book to release this panic inside of you. I had to try it. I was so exhausted trying to manage my chronic anxiety. I went into meditation and visualized the tiger he described in the book. The idea was to imagine that moment that tiger was attacking you. In that primal state of fear and panic you then release that tiger and get away from it. You tell yourself you are safe. It worked. The concept was that you finally released the 'fight or flight' adrenaline because you told your primordial body that you were safe. Another book I highly recommend if you are dealing with anxiety. It was incredibly beneficial to me during this time and since.

"As surely as we hear the blood in our ears, the echoes of a million midnight shrieks of monkeys, whose last sight of the world was the eyes of a panther, have their traces in our nervous systems." Paul Shepard

?s=digital-text&ie=UTF8&qid=1524162806&sr=1-1&keywords=waking +the+tiger

When I was dealing with candida and parasites in 2011 the diet was almost enough to bring me back to a strong state. I remember that by the time I started taking herbs to eliminate the parasites I had barely any symptoms and even though I was just beginning to kill the parasites it felt like a breeze. The mold detox was not as easy. It took several weeks of disciplined diet and detoxing to get myself into a space where I could even walk for a period of time. I remember two particular instances where I thought I was really getting better but then even applying myself a small amount made me exhausted. The first instance was when I decided I was well enough to go for a walk. There was a small hiking trail behind my apartment. I loved it because when you got to the top of the hill you could see the entire city skyline. It was beautiful. It was so nice outside and I felt like I was missing the entire summer. I put on my sneakers and went outside. It was so good to be in the fresh air! There were a few pine trees near my door and the smell in the summer sun was refreshing. I put on my headphones and decided to play a Tibetan Buddhist Monk playlist[32]. The chanting soothed me. I listened to many chants over the course of all of my illnesses and even now that I am well. There is a lot of power in chanting; both listening and doing it yourself. By the time I made it past the fence to even get on the trail (this was about 50 feet) I was ready to lie down. I couldn't believe how much it took out of me! But I also knew that walking or any form of exercise opens the lymph and allows for detoxification. I knew that my body was likely releasing toxins and so I needed to keep going.

I made it to the top of the hill. I was completely exhausted and felt a little out of sorts, but I had made it. I could feel the numbness coming back into my legs, so I knew I had likely pushed a little too hard. I also knew that I was clearing energy. That is the hard part about any kind of detox. You have to keep going and trust your intuition and the guidelines given by your doctor. Even when the symptoms were magnified and even when I thought I would never get well I just kept going. I trusted my doctor when she said there is a light at the end of the tunnel. Perseverance is key.

---

[32] Tibetan Mantras for Turbulent Times http://devapremalmiten.com/tibetan-mantras-for-turbulent-times/

The second instance was 4th of July. This was after a full month of binders and the mold diet. The major symptoms were dissipating. I was still very imbalanced when it came to my thyroid swings, but I had a lot of my physical energy back. I remember going with one of my best friends downtown for the fireworks display. Not only was I exhausted walking to where we were sitting but I also was very overwhelmed by all the people. And it was hot! Because of my thyroid issue I could not stand the heat! Being hot also seemed to make my hand curl and my hair fall out. This was awful. In fact, I remember also driving in the summer heat and having to pull over because my anger started to rage, and my hair started falling out in clumps. Seriously, this crazy stuff happened.

By August 1st I had been out of work for about 3 months. I had also been on CSM for about 2 months and saw incredibly process on the vision test for mold. I knew it was time to go back to work. I got a job at a women's apparel store. It was actually the first store I ever worked for back in 1998 as a retail manager. I was so excited to be back there. It was like coming home. It gave me comfort and it also provided some safety and security I desperately needed to feel. They were flexible with my health issues and allowed me to start back part time while I got my strength back. At this time, I had lost another 20 pounds through the diet and illness. I thought; at least I look good!

The next month went by quickly and before I knew it I was really feeling well. I started to work full days and I was taking less and less of the L Carnitine for my thyroid. I had an intuitive hit that as soon as I could stop taking the CSM I would be able to go off the L Carnitine and start rebalancing my thyroid. I was praying I could salvage it. In the meantime, I had a system for when I needed to take it and how much and it seemed to be working. By September of 2016 I was working full time and managing my own store again. I was still on a strict diet, but I had finally tested green on both eyes on the mold vision test and was able to go off of CSM. Finally! I was able to switch to charcoal and clay binders which I still take every day to this day. But now it is for maintenance and not for major detoxification. I took Ashwaganda for my thyroid all the way through December, but the gravelly voice finally left me at the end of the year and today I am Hashimoto's free.

Dealing with mold was intense. It was also such a blessing because it revealed to me the final pieces of my health puzzle. I now have all the information that I need to properly take care of myself. I am forever grateful to my doctor who knew exactly what was wrong with me and was able to save me. I am forever grateful to my spiritual practice because it was what supported my discipline and my faith to persevere. There are people that die each day from autoimmune disease, exposure to mold and toxins and other bizarre illness that western medicine just cannot explain. The information is getting out there but there needs to be more. I leave you here with; you can heal! You can get better! It's possible to completely overcome what you are fighting.

It takes a willingness to become aware. Through spiritual practice and disciplines like meditation and self-inquiry you will come to see your authentic self and begin to remove the toxic energies in your life that have taken you out of alignment. You must also become wise. You must gather the data about your physical body and how it functions. The following section shares information on all that I have learned in understanding how my own body functions. The key note here is that everyone is different. The information I share are guidelines for diet and detoxification as it relates to mold, candida and the MTHFR mutation. Gather all of your own data from your team of health professionals before you make any major changes. I am not re-inventing any diets here either. Throughout the Become Wise section you will find websites and resources that will help you with diet and supplementation. I have now been an active experiment for these diets and detoxification practices and what I share in the following section are the key learnings from that experimentation and research.

BECOME WISE

PURIFY. ENERGIZE. HEAL

11

Diet Basics

Candida Diet

Candida is a pathogen in our body. We all have Candida albicans[33] in our body. If you have taken antibiotics, birth control or have issues with digestion you likely have a candida overgrowth. There are great resources that go into depth with candida; www.thecandidadiet.org is the best resource I can think to recommend. It is full of information and recipes to support those suffering from candida overgrowth. Western medicine does not recognize the overgrowth because there is no way to test for it. Because every human has candida in their system; anyone who tests for it will be positive. It is important to partner with a doctor who practices functional and/or integrative medicine that understands how candida can affect the body and how to overcome it. There is a questionnaire on www.thecandidadiet.org that you can take to see if you may have candida overgrowth. The link to the questionnaire is https://www.thecandidadiet.com/candida-questionnaire/.

---

[33] *Candida albicans* is an opportunistic pathogenic yeast that is a common member of the human gut flora. It does not proliferate outside the human body. It is detected in the gastrointestinal tract and mouth in 40-60% of healthy adults. It is usually a commensalorganism, but can become pathogenic in immunocompromised individuals under a variety of conditions. It is one of the few species of the *Candida* genus that causes the human infection candidiasis, which results from an overgrowth of the fungus. https://en.wikipedia.org/wiki/Candida_albicans

The Candida diet is a diet with no sugar. Zero sugar. The object of the diet is to remove sugar which feeds the candida pathogen which is a form of yeast. If you eat any amount of sugar, even if you want to have some fruit, it can cause the yeast to grow and your symptoms immediately return. The diet starves the yeast and your body processes the die off out. Die-off are the toxins that are produced when the candida dies in your body. Have you ever made bread? When you add warm water to yeast it begins to die. It produces gas when it ferments which is what makes bread dough rise. Those gases are a direct representation of what is happening in your body. Those gases can have quite an effect which is why the diet can be so challenging. You are not only managing sugar cravings, but you are also managing the toxins that are rising in your system.

There are a few different approaches to the Candida diet. The first approach is to go hard core right out of the gate. That means cut out ALL sugar and eat an alkalized diet consisting of green vegetables and protein. Typically, some symptoms from the candida disappear quickly and you start to feel much better. This is followed by the detox flu where you may have sinus issues, feel nauseous, headaches etc. The spiral that some people get into with this diet is that they start to feel better and don't want the horrible die off symptoms and end up not following through on the diet. It is so important to FOLLOW THROUGH. It should take at least thirty days to eliminate most of the candida overgrowth and even after that period you may need to continue the diet to eliminate yeast. It took me over 6 months to clear it out of my system and return it to a balanced or 'normal' yeast amount.

Another approach to the diet is to be subtle with it. If you aren't experiencing chronic symptoms but you want to detox excess yeast from your body, you can start by just doing a slow elimination of sugar and build up to the hard core zero sugar diet. This reduces the amount of detox flu symptoms you may have while you are still supporting your system.

My advice or recommended approach is to go 'all in' with your diet but be subtle building up probiotics and antifungals. Eliminate ALL sugar from your diet so yeast can no longer grow in your body. The symptoms of yeast die off are typically nausea, headaches, sinus congestion and fatigue. Brain fog can also be a problem. However, brain fog can be a problem when you are having trouble with yeast, so it may be an issue either way. The good news is that after 30 days on the diet the brain fog starts to lift and often times can be clear altogether. There can be many more symptoms, but this is the most common. After you cut out sugar it is time to notice how you are feeling. How soon do you have die off? And for how long? My die off symptoms came in waves. I would have a really bad day where I felt terrible and exhausted and then the next day feel great. My cycle was about every 3 days. After one month of the diet I noticed that I didn't have the die off symptoms. This is how you know to go to the next step.

Once you have your yeast under control through diet you need to start hitting it even harder with probiotics and antifungals. I am going to go into specifics in the Detox section on what kinds of probiotics are best, but I will talk about antifungals here. The best antifungals to start with are natural ones; Garlic, Oregano Oil, Candidase, GSE are just a few of the good ones. Follow the instructions for these antifungals. You may want to try a few different ones to see what works best for you. You also may want to rotate which antifungals you are taking to ensure that you are hitting the candida from every direction. It is important to drink a lot of water and to notice if you start to have major die off symptoms again. You want to build up your antifungals from a small amount to the max the directions say to take so that you continue to stay balanced and manage through the die off cycle.

Mold Diet

The mold diet[34] is a diet that is low in mycotoxins. It is also a diet free of mold and fungus. This means no mushrooms and no blue cheese. It means you do not eat anything that may sit for long periods of time, has been fermented or has been in contact with wet moldy environments.

---

[34] Two great resources for the Mold Diet are: https://www.bulletproof.com/ and https://www.jillcarnahan.com/2015/02/08/low-mold-diet/

The major things to be aware of here is that dairy is out; this includes any fermented cheese. You want to stay away from nuts that are high in mold; peanuts, pistachios and cashews are the top of that list. You want to stick to almonds, hazelnuts, coconuts, pecans and walnuts. You also want to stay away from beans; garbanzo beans, pinto beans, any sprouted legumes. Melon is very high in mold content. So is corn, soy and any dried fruits. Watch out here for any processed gluten free items as well. There are some brands that are great for my system and others that I can't eat at all. Lastly, coffee and chocolate can be very high in mycotoxins. A bummer I know, but I can tell you that there are excellent brands of organic coffees and chocolate that is produced in a way that they minimize mold and produce a low mycotoxin product. There is hope for all you chocolate lovers out there!

If you are sensitive to mold you will notice when you eat something that bothers you. For those who know they have mold issues in their genetics (or even if you have discovered it on your own) you will know how mold makes you feel. I get dizzy when I eat or drink anything high in mycotoxins. I have to stay away from certain coffee shops and certain brands and sometimes you eat at a restaurant and realize you just are going to have to get through the night feeling off track. So be careful!

A big different from candida detox and mold detox is you use binders, like charcoal, to remove toxins from your body when you have a mold issue. I had to go through the candida diet 5 years before I went through the mold diet. I have to say the mold diet uncovered a really cool piece of the puzzle! All of those die off symptoms I was talking about are actually minimized by taking a binder! I read so many forums where people were suffering from horrible die off and didn't know how to get through it. I was excited to learn about charcoal and clay because they bind toxins and remove them from your body. This allows you to have a lot less die off symptoms and a lot less stress when you are eliminating mold toxins and candida from your body. The side effect of taking binders, such as charcoal, is that the toxin is re-exposed to your body as it is being removed. This means you can often become more ill or have your symptoms magnified as they are being removed.

12

Detox and Probiotics

I imagine that after reading about the candida and mold diets that you may be asking yourself; why the heck would I want to go through any of that? I know it sounds awful. I won't lie to you; the process can be awful. It can be scary and hard, and you may feel like you just want to give up. But if you can stay disciplined with the diet and you support your detox properly; you WILL get through it! Just don't wait. Don't wait to do this for yourself. I had to be near death before I went through these diet plans. And not once but twice! Don't wait until your health, your weight, your mental well-being and your overall enjoyment of life is nearly gone before you decide to get healthy and do something about the symptoms that are lurking. I say lurking because they are usually so subtle and build over time. It isn't until something really stops working properly before we think to act. You don't gain 100 pounds overnight and you don't become sick overnight - well not always anyways. I can also tell you that it is worth the discipline. It is worth sticking to the plan and getting through the hard symptoms because you do wake up one day and feel better. The fog does lift and the weight comes off and the symptoms start to dissipate and you may feel better than you have ever felt!

Probiotics

When you start to eat a clean diet it is so important to start taking strong probiotics. Here are my suggestions when choosing a probiotic[35]:

- If it's not alive and kept cold in a refrigerated space than it is not going to do anything for you. A probiotic that it is on the shelf will likely not make it past your stomach to reach your gut where it really needs it. When you do buy them; keep them cold.
- Make sure that it has over a billion CFUs. About half of the probiotic will die in your stomach. In this case there is power in the numbers. The more probiotic in a cap the more likely it will reach your intestines where you really need them to populate your gut.
- It needs to be multiple strands. One strand isn't enough. There are probiotic strands that will populate your sinuses and others that populate other parts of your gut. You need to have more than one strand because you have more than one microorganism living in your body.
- Start with one cap a day - preferably on an empty stomach. You want to build up to 3 or 4 caps a day depending on the probiotic. Always read the instructions and ask your doctor if you have questions.

Detox

The following are my tips to support your detox.

- Charcoal[36] and Clay[37] - these are binders that you take to remove toxins. You want to take them on empty stomachs. They bind

---

[35] I recommend Kaire Labs Detox Support https://www.amazon.com/gp/product/B0057ZEDCO/ref=oh_aui_detailpage_o00_s00?ie=UTF8&psc=1
[36] Bulletproof Coconut Charcoal https://www.bulletproof.com/coconut-charcoal-capsules-90-ct
[37] GI Detox https://www.amazon.com/Detox-Cleanse-Capsules-Botanical-Research/dp/B009KT9TEU/ref=sr_1_4_s_it?s=hpc&ie=UTF8&qid=1523813360&sr=1-4&keywords=GI+detox

whatever is in your stomach so if you take them with food or other supplements they will just pull those out. That is a waste of money! You want the binder to pull out excess toxins in your body. I recommend Bulletproof charcoal, but any activated coconut charcoal will work. I take 4-8 caps a day, but you can take as little as 1-2. I would start with one and see if you have any symptoms within an hour. If not, the next time you take them jump to 2. I take my charcoal at night before bed, sometimes first thing in the morning and in between meals. Just make sure it is 2 hours after and before you eat or take anything else. You can certainly drink water or tea with them.

- Infrared Sauna - This really helped me with my mold detox. I went and sat in an infrared sauna 3 times a week to remove heavy metals and toxins from my body. It is highly effective and removes a much higher percentage of toxins in one sitting than a regular dry sauna. That said, do use a dry sauna whenever you get a chance. Stay away from a steam room though. Steam rooms or wet steam is usually full of mold and supports mold and fungus growth. It can make things worse for you if you are trying to remove mold and fungus from your body.

- Lymph Brushing - This works! You can get a lymph brush just about anywhere that sells bath products these days. You can also google how to brush. The important part is to brush towards the heart from all your lymph. If you do this every single shower, then you will support the detoxing of the lymph nodes.

- Cold shower/Hot Shower - after you lymph brush in the shower; end it with a cold hit. Turn the shower to as cool as you can stand it before you get out and then shut it off. This shocks the immune system and helps it to boost up in power.

- Drink LOTS of water. I also add Electrolytes to my water. Just make sure its sugar free. The more electrolytes the better because you may experience cotton mouth when detoxing from mold and the electrolytes help restore balance of salt in your body.

- Yoga for the Lymph system - There are lots of good postures for your lymphatic system. My favorite is to lay flat on your back and then kick your legs up over your head and hold them there for a few minutes. This flushes your lymphatic system. The more you can support the flushing of your lymphatic system the better because it decreases your chances of dealing with additional infections arising as the toxins are clearing out of your body.

– Stay disciplined! The most important thing is to not give up and stick to detoxing your body. You may experience all kinds of symptoms while you are detoxing, and you may also have cravings. I would tell myself; it's the yeast that wants that sugar, not me. I would repeat this as a daily mantra until I finally got through the cravings.

– Keep your body alkaline. Your body becomes highly acidic if you are removing toxins from your body. Use PH strips to text your urine to see if you are acidic. If you eat more green vegetables and drink more water. You can also take grasses by PHIon[38] that will alkalize your system. The more alkaline you are the less likely you will be overcome by disease. It also helps your body to process out the toxins with far less inflammation. Remember acidity equals inflammation.

– If you are detoxing from mold, fungus or candida you may experience thyroid issues, like Hashimoto's, or adrenal crashes. My advice to get through these is twofold. First, rest. Listen to your body and rest. The exhaustion will not last forever. Second, do some research on herbs to support your thyroid and adrenals and give some a try. I recommend Endoflex by Young Living Oils to help with the adrenals and overall endocrine health. For thyroid support I recommend Ashwaganda as a supplement to balance the thyroid. I was lucky that those were enough to bring me into balance. That said, please partner with your functional medicine doctor to find what's right for you.

---

[38] https://www.phionbalance.com/

13

Food Basics

Folate Rich, Low Mycotoxin diet for those who also suffer from Candida or Sugar issues

Protein

Grass Fed Beef, Lamb or Bison
Wild Caught Fish
Pastured Eggs or Fresh Farm Eggs
Pastured Pork or Chicken

When it comes to protein you want the best quality meats that you can manage within your budget and location. If you can eat local farm fresh ingredients that is best. Grass fed, wild caught and pasture raised reduce and/or eliminate (in most cases) the use of antibiotics, processed foods fed to the animal, and mycotoxins. A lot of large plants raising cattle and other animals may feed them corn. Corn is extremely high in mycotoxins because it sits in silos and grain stores and becomes moldy. If you can stick to grass-fed you reduce that risk significantly.

It is important to stay away from fish that are high in mercury. The best fish options are; wild caught salmon and trout, haddock, sole and flounder.

Minimize the use of egg yolks. If you are allergic to dairy you will find that your reaction is higher to the yolks than the whites. It is still good to have a balance but when you can do egg whites it is a better option.

Vegetables

High Folate Vegetables:
Dark Leafy Greens
Asparagus
Broccoli
Lentils*
Avocado
Brussel Sprouts
Bok Choy
Cauliflower*
Cucumber
Kale
Spinach
Celery
Squash
Zucchini

*Watch the acidity in cauliflower and Lentils. If you are in the die-off portion of the candida detox you may be too acidic, and these particular vegetables may affect your energy levels.

Eat as many green leafy vegetables as you want. They alkalize the body and they are high in Folate. They will support you through any detox and will keep your energy levels high. Avocado is excellent for the nervous system and is a great source of folate, vitamins and quality fat. If you are experiencing anxiety from the detox or you just aren't sure what to eat; sometimes an avocado is enough to fill you up for a few hours and calms you at the same time.

You want to stay away from most beans because of their mycotoxin levels. Like corn, beans are usually left to sit in food stores and they become moldy leaving a high level of mycotoxins.

Other great vegetables:

Carrots
Radishes
Artichokes
Green onion
Beets
Pumpkin

The main vegetable to stay away from is corn. Corn is high in mycotoxins and sugars. They do not support the candida diet nor a mold diet.

I also want to note here that Beets, Carrots and squash like butternut and acorn are too high in sugar if you are on the first portion of the detox from candida. You do not want to eat these unless you are relieved of the majority of your candida symptoms.

Fruit

Avocado
Blackberries and Raspberries
Cranberries
Coconut
Citrus
Blueberries
Pineapple
Strawberries
Grapefruit
Green Apples

*Stay away from all melon. It is high in sugar and mold therefore mycotoxins. Also stay away from bananas and grapes as they are extremely high in sugar. Dried fruit carries a high level of mycotoxins because of how the fruit is processed and is also extremely high in sugar and should be avoided.

If you stick to fruits that are natural antioxidants such as the berries and citrus listed above you should be in good shape. If you are on the candida detox diet you should not eat any fruit. You want to get through the first 30 days of detox before you add fruit into your diet. Fruits simply still have too much sugar if you are fighting candida.

Beverages

Water
Low Mycotoxin Coffee
Green Tea
Coconut Milk
Almond Milk
Mineral Water

Stay away from Soy Milk because it can impact your hormones. Stay away from Cashew Milk products because Cashews are high in Mold.

You have to do your research to better understand how to pinpoint coffee that is low in mycotoxins. You have to find a grower and roaster who does not allow their beans to sit for long period of time when they can get moldy. There are two brands I highly recommend; Bulletproof Coffee and Kicking Horse Coffee. Look for organic coffees and do your research on the company and their process before you buy it.

Alcohol is not recommended. If you are not in the midst of a detox I would stick to plant-based alcohols like Tequila or Potato Vodka. Potatoes are high in sugar, so Tequila is your best option. Drink wisely.

Fruit juice is also not recommended because it is extremely high in sugar and over-processed.

Starch

Starch is tricky. White potatoes are a no go. Stay away from them. Sweet potatoes are okay but just like beets, carrots and some squash you want to limit it if you are in the early stages of fighting candida.

Brown rice is best if you are on the candida diet, but it is high in mycotoxins. White rice is lower in mycotoxins but high in sugar. My doctor recommends white or brown jasmine rice. It is low in sugar and in mycotoxins compared to most. It is a great source of sugar too when you are not able to have anything else.

Quinoa is okay but really all other starches can be challenging for 'moldy's'.

One thing I want to share here. Edgar Cayce was a famous channel and he received a lot of information from Spirit about dead that has been scientifically proven to be effective. One thing I learned from researching his work is that it is really important to eat starch separately from protein. Your body has a difficult time processing those two things together. The best way to eat your rice is to eat it after dinner as a dessert. Eat your dinner of vegetables and protein and then about an hour or two later; eat a bowl of rice with some clarified butter. I love to put Cinnamon and Garam Masala in it too. When you can't have sugar, it can be a delicious dessert. It also helps you sleep to eat rice before bed and can give you great energy if you have gone days without sugar. One rice that I recommend is truroots[39] brown rice with GaBa. It's great for reducing anxiety and tastes delicious too.

Oils and Fats

I use clarified butter or Ghee almost always when I cook. I also use coconut oil and grass-fed butter. Stay away from Canola Oil or other processed oils.

Herbs and Spices

You can really use any herbs and spices you want but I want to highlight some that really support your immune system.

Turmeric
Paprika

---

[39] https://www.truroots.com/products/truroots-originals

Cayenne
Curry
Garam Masala
Cinnamon
Basil
Cilantro
Parsley
Sea Salt
Don'ts
Soy and Whey Proteins
Dairy

It's good to stay away from Dairy altogether but I will note that fresh goat or sheep's milk cheese don't bother me as long as I eat it in moderation. Those fresh cheeses are a treat every once in a while. Stay away from cow's milk and cheese as much as possible. I eat coconut yogurt and ice cream and it tastes amazing!

14

Folate Fundamentals

After all this discussion about diet and food there is still a third component to how I eat that I want to share with you. In addition to eating to eliminate candida, mold and fungus from my body; I also have to eat foods high in folate.

One quarter of the population has some form of a genetic mutation that hinders your body's ability to process folate correctly. This mutation is the MTHFR[40] genetic mutation. There are two major forms and you can be tested for these by your doctor or by using 23andme. I am double heterozygous which means I have both forms of the mutation. I am not a doctor or a scientist, so I will not go into the depth on this that is possible. However, I will tell you that there is a lot of good information out there now. I will summarize this with what I know. I know that i cannot process Folic Acid. The more Folic Acid I intake the sicker I can become. This can actually lead to autoimmune diseases as serious as MS or Lupus. My body can also run low in B12 which can hinder this process further. Methyl Folate or MTHFR does so many things for your body. It helps you to methylate or remove toxins from the body and it also helps you to rebuild your cells. Without proper amounts of folate, you can be ill more frequently or even have serious issues. My MTHFR mutation is the likely cause of my miscarriage a few years ago. It is actually common to be tested if you have a miscarriage. It is

---

[40] For more information on MTHFR https://www.jillcarnahan.com/2013/05/12/mthfr-gene-mutation-whats-the-big-deal-about-methylation/

unfortunate that it takes something serious for a doctor to test for it. This is why a good doctor is so important.

Some of the general rules of thumb when you have the MTHFR mutation:

- Stay clear of heavy metals even when you are cooking. Try to use ceramic or stainless steel.
- Eat lots of green leafy vegetables
- Avoid folic acid. It's in everything. Check your vitamin labels too.
- B vitamins are critical. Take a good B complex. Make sure it has Folate or L-5 Folate. Do NOT take any vitamins that have Folate as Folic Acid or Folic Acid.
- Eat a low grain diet

15

Vitamins 101

Vitamins are very important. Our body can become deficient in certain vitamins and it can really throw you off track. Gathering data about your body is an important part of the 'Become Wise' phase of your health. Your doctor can check your vitamin levels on critical vitamins. It is good to get a baseline if you can, so you know where you may need more support. It is best to take your vitamins separately as a single source of one kind of vitamin rather than having them grouped together in a multivitamin. There is a lot of good research on supplements and vitamins. I recommend reading The Bulletproof Diet for an easy to read guide. I don't want to get into all the research and recommend you learn about your own body and what feels right to you. That said, I want to share my recommendations as must do's when it comes to vitamins.

- Do not take a multivitamin. You are just peeing your vitamins out in the toilet. There is a lot in a multivitamin that you may not need and there is almost always Folic Acid in a multivitamin tablet.
- Take Vitamin C (up to 1 gram a day), Vitamin D3 (5000 IU's per day), B complex, B12 in addition to the complex, Methyl Folate may be needed but partner with your doctor on that one.
- Take a probiotic

- Take Zinc or a Zinc Complex. I recommend New Chapter Organics Zinc Supplement[41]

If you partner with a good functional medicine doctor and you do your own research, you will find what works best to support your system. The basics above support all the necessary components of your immune system so you can boost your system while going through a detox plan.

---

[41] New Chapter Organics Zinc Complex https://www.amazon.com/New-Chapter -Zinc-Supplement-Ingredients/dp/B0015R2TCO/ref=sr_1_1_a_it ?ie=UTF8&qid=1523813730&sr=8-1&keywords=new+chapter+organics+zinc+ supplement

16

Food Allergies

It is very important to begin to understand what foods are serving you and what foods are not. Most of us have food sensitivities and/or food allergies. There are foods that make our bodies bloat, foods that cause diarrhea and some foods that also make us feel strong or give us extra energy. It is important to begin to build a relationship with your food. By knowing what works for your body and what doesn't; you will begin to understand how to 'feed' your body properly and will eliminate the constant up and down cycle created by eating food that creates negative vibrations in your system.

You have already started your food journal with all of the exercises we have completed. This next portion is an addition to the emotional journaling you have been documenting. It is time to keep track of what and when you are eating to better understand how food affects you physically and emotionally. I have included template for one day of food journaling to start to understand your food sensitivities in addition to your emotional eating patterns. I recommend you complete this daily for a minimum of one week, so you can begin to see your patterns. It is best to keep track for 30 days to best understand your food reactions and emotional eating patterns.

Begin to notice patterns of behavior; i.e. I was stressed so I ate a cookie, or I feel bloated each time I eat cheese. Through food journaling you will begin to see how to change your diet to nurture your body vs. punish it.

There are many belief systems around nutrition and diet. I will say that it is important to begin to eliminate those things that make you feel unwell. There is a significant amount of people in the United States who have become Gluten and Dairy intolerant. When working with individual clients I recommend eliminating these items from your diet completely in addition to allergy testing and supplement regimes.

Lastly, knowledge is power. If you can afford the testing for food allergies I highly recommend it. Having true data about your body is always the best route. If you keep a proper food journal you truly don't need to go through the testing. But if you are like me you will want the black and white facts. My recommendation is to have the blood work done through a Functional Medicine doctor. Western medicine testing is not as advanced as what is available in functional medicine and often times is not as accurate.

Spend time watching your behaviors and becoming aware of your physical body and its needs. You should gain a much better perspective on what has been working for you and what you need to change. The goal here is to come into relationship with your body and your food. This relationship will empower you to nourish yourself.

Food Sensitivity Tracking Template

Date:

Today I ate:

```
```

How did I feel after I ate? How did my physical body feel?

How did I feel before I ate? Was there something occurring in my life that was causing me to eat?

Physical Reactions:

```
```

What foods have you decided to eliminate from your diet because of how they affect your body?

What emotional and/or outside triggers caused you to eat or not eat?

As you tracked you're eating habits What did you learn about your eating habits?

Some Homework

Wow! You've come a long way from where you started. Now is the time for some homework to help review all the steps that you have been taking and continue your food journal and exercise regime. Stop everything and before you go to the last chapter please complete the following activity and self-inquiry questions.

Activity 1. Go back to the body of glass and this time; ask to see your energy systems. Take note of where there are blocks that may be causing stalled energy in your field and in fact are creating weight.

Journal Entry

How do I feel about my progress over the past few weeks?

What goals have I accomplished? Where am I still stuck?

What would I like to see transform over the next 8 weeks as I continue to put these tools into practice?

Where do I feel I still need support?

What can I learn about myself from this?

What has been my 'aha' moment around my 'weight'?

17

Putting it all Together

I have been awake for awhile now.

*I have seen what I have accepted for my-self and the cost has been great.
I have felt the Oneness of Truth and felt the
Purity of Joy for the first time.
I have lost friends and lovers, homes and pets.
I have gained Teachers, Colleagues and Soul Mates.
I have learned how to Trust and have accepted my-
self as the proverbial Fool, who goes on trusting, even
when I have been abused, lied to and cheated.
I have scraped layers of grief, anger and despair off my
body as one scrapes a worn sticker off a windshield.
I have danced, laughed and played.
I remember what it was like to be a child even
when I have no recollection of it.
I have forgiven past hurts, healed relationships and have
seen as some friends leave me; others are coming back.
I have come to understand the importance
of Truth, Authenticity and Self.
I have learned that no matter how difficult a situation can
be that if embraced, it can bring healing to many.
I have re-connected.
I have seen as my 'literal' weight is falling off, the
emotional weight is revealed, cleared and purified.*

I have been awake for awhile now.

I am still learning about my-self.
I am still trying to understand it all.
I am not certain of my future but certain that I
create my future here in the present.
I see. I see you, God and My-Self.
We all look the same.
I feel everything and nothing.
I pause, reflect and listen; noticing what I never noticed before.

I am awake.

Recapitulation is defined as an act or instance of summarizing and restating the main points of something. A more favorable definition is the repetition of an evolutionary or other kind of process during development or growth. I have had three very specific moments of recapitulation. In therapy it may be called a break through. It is a moment where new information comes to light about your life that casts all the past experiences in a new light. More than that, it puts all of your memories in perfect order, so you have a full understanding of how you came to be. It is an incredible experience, miraculous really, to suddenly understand the why's to all that has happened in your life. Two of these major turning points were due to the illness' I have described that brought me near death. I believe that so many layers of the lotus blossom of my life were revealed because of my willingness to look within and 'do the work' of self-reflection. I also believe that everyone has the right to have this same gift of healing. It is with right action and the willingness to reflect on oneself that you are able to unlock the potential of your spirit and heal yourself in all realms; physical, spiritual and emotional.

It is with all of my diagnoses; candida overgrowth, parasites, food allergies, MTHFR Mutation, Autoimmune disease, Lyme's Disease and CIRS that everything I had ever suffered from was fully explained. I had chronic tonsillitis and had my tonsils removed at the age of 5. I had chronic ear infections all throughout Elementary School and Junior High. I battled my weight. I threw up after eating ice cream and had unexplained rashes and fungal infections. I have had pneumonia 5 different times in my life. I struggled with cystic acne and would often be very acidic and gassy to the point I went through a year period where I threw up acid every morning. These strange bouts of illness with unexplained symptoms.

My immune system was compromised due to my genetics. This made me susceptible to infection at a young age. The infections led to an overuse of antibiotics. The antibiotics led to a decline in my body's probiotics which led to yeast overgrowth. That led to unexpected weight gain and constant sugar cravings. I also drank milk and ate dairy products. Because of my bodies reaction to them it made me retain water adding even more weight and led to constant gas and bloating. Because I could not methylate properly the toxins from my environment and from the candida overgrowth in my body I started having cystic acne and my face would be red and my skin was never clear. My sinuses and ears were full of fungus, not bacteria, but because we didn't know that I was given antibiotics to clear the bacteria portion of the infection that was actually stemming from the fungal infection. When we moved from an older home (that was covered in moss and was in a wet environment) to a new home many of my symptoms ceased. I was removed from a moldy environment and I went through a period of 3 years without antibiotics and chronic sinus and ear infections. During that time period my weight and hormones balanced out and I was feeling quite good by the time I graduated high school.

Throughout my 20's I took birth control and did not take proper care of my health. I also ate whatever I wanted, and my diet consisted of French cooking by my now ex-husband who was a French chef and fast food. All of my food choices were rich with dairy and wheat. Between the birth control and the diet, I gained over 100 pounds in that ten-year period. I also was having issues with my cycle and my hormones because of the MTHFR mutation and taking in too much folic acid and accruing additional toxins. I miscarried because of the

MTHFR mutation. I became exhausted, did not have my cycle and was extremely emotional as well as overweight. By the time I left my marriage I weighed 247 pounds and was unwell. I was able to save myself only slightly by leaving my marriage and beginning to exercise and eliminating the dairy rich French foods, but it was not enough. I had a bout of pneumonia that nearly put me in the hospital and whatever I ate that exposed me to the parasites...well the parasites went rampant in my body. I had three parasites; one was in my liver, one in my mouth and sinuses, and the third was systemic and came from water - likely from my trips to Hawaii. This all led to my first near-death and illness in 2011.

The candida diet and detox I went through to get well in 2011 kept me well for the next 5 years. But it did not keep me vital. I still struggled. The apartment I lived in Boulder was in an area that had been flooded the year before and was infested with black mold. The black mold triggered my CIRS and it created all of the neurological symptoms, panic and anxiety and the swelling in my head. When I left Boulder, these symptoms ceased until I moved to Maui in 2014 and then the mold and fungus in the tropical environment triggered the symptoms to return. These symptoms never really went completely away after I returned to the dry state of Colorado and they flared up as mysterious symptoms all throughout the next two years until the mold on the cat triggered a massive attack. With all of this explained I was finally able to pull 37 years of toxins out of my body and start restoring my health to its full capacity. Yes, I do have to take multiple supplements every day and I do have to follow a strict diet. Yes, I do have mold symptoms reappear when I am exposed to moldy environments. I am very sensitive to mold and fungus in food and in the environment. But with all these issues presented I am able to manage my health holistically and through diet. I have regained my full energy; my hair and I am living in better health than I ever have in my life. Even when I catch a cold or get sick with a virus my recovery time is half what is used to be.

I have so much gratitude for the information that has been revealed to me. It has not only given me the courage to overcome but it has put in order all of the health challenges I have had in my life. It freed me from feeling 'crazy' which is what was put upon me when I would explain my symptoms. This book has been an incredible journey and we have made it to the end! At this time, you should have achieved a greater awareness of your body and your emotions. You have begun the journey of building a relationship with food and your physical being. You have figured out what foods work for you and which don't. You have begun a meditation practice and an exercise routine.

What's next?

What's next is up to you. I have given you some basic tools to use in your daily life and have offered self-inquiry exercises to inspire your mind to open to what is really going on inside. It's up to you to continue to use these tools and build upon them in order to experience continued success in your physical, emotional and spiritual health.

Now that you have discovered some of the foods that affect your body in a toxic way and/or create inflammation; continue to remove those foods from your daily routine. Keep your food journal handy so you can continue to document how you feel when you eat. Continue to talk to your body. Ask your body daily; what do you need from me? As you continue to change your diet; it may now be time to partner with your physician or chosen healer and begin to look at food allergies, or dietary needs that work with your body and specific blood type. And last but most important; pay attention to your emotions! Your emotional state is the unlock to most of your physical ailments. By being in tune with your emotions and working through them; even expressing them, you will find your physical well-being stays in balance and it is easier to manage your day to day routines.

Remember the process of healing is timeless and consists of 4 key areas.

Become aware – Come out of Samsara. Be willing to complete self-inquiry exercises. Practice mindfulness.

Become wise – Find the teachers, doctors and healers that you trust that can help you to begin your journey. Find out as much information as you can about your body and yourself. Learn all you can. Study different spiritual practices and find what works for you. Take different exercise courses to find what works for you. Read and Study.

Practice - You must practice all that you are learning. Meditating and practicing mindfulness daily. The more you practice the more solid you become in your Self and your Spirit. The practice is The Path and The Way.

TRUST – Faith is the most important piece. You have to trust in yourself and in the Divine. You have to trust that you are always safe in the hands of Spirit. When you do not trust you must go back to the beginning with self-inquiry. What is it that I do not trust?

About the Author

Toxicity is surfacing at an ever-increasing rate to be purified and released so global consciousness can continue to expand. On a personal level, we also are being called to purify our bodies and minds to reach new levels of awareness. Over the past decade I have been blessed to work with many different clients, including my own personal journey, to remove toxic energies from our lives and fine tune our vibration. For me the result has been a physical loss of over 100 pounds and a completely new direction in work and relationships.

Spiritual and psychic gifts came to me through the generations of women in my family. I am the fourth generation of an incredible group of gifted healers, mediums and channels. I am able to give guidance to help heal your life through psychic readings, visiting the Akashic Records, connecting to teachers and loved ones and journeying to different Lokas or dimensions specialize in helping you transition out of or recover from toxic situations such as; toxic work environments, home environments, toxic relationships and food sensitivities and toxicities. We will work together to identify the spiritual and emotional cause of attraction of these negative situations and begin to heal them through soul retrieval, self-inquiry and spiritual practices.

I have a personal relationship with mold toxins and fungus. Their metaphysical reason to exist in a body is holding on to your past and allowing toxic energies to feed on your energy. For me, this was a direct correlation to the toxic relationships I had built and my own food addiction and patterns of codependency. I have found there are many sensitives managing these same issues. I have a special program for those of you suffering from mold and fungus dysfunction. This involves detox support for your physical body as well as emotional support as you move through the detox. The most important piece is using self-inquiry to identify the areas in your childhood that may have created these patterns; such as childhood abuse or addictive behaviors in your family. Once these areas are identified we are able to journey back to those ages and complete soul retrieval to begin to bring these fragments back to your Self to become whole.

It is my passion to cultivate compassion and loving kindness and it is through my Faith in the teachers and Gurus that I have been able to be healed. I now offer service to you, so we can all live in balance, health and vitality and increase conscious awareness for the greater good of all sentient beings.

Lisa has an Associates of Applied Science Degree in Culinary Arts from the Art Institute of Colorado and is certified in Nutritional Cooking by the American Culinary Federation; Recognized by the National Association of Psychics and Mediums, Ordained Minister through the Universal Life Church and is a Certified Professional Tarot Reader through the Tarot Certification Board of America. Lisa also completed the Berkeley Psychic Institute's Program through Psychic Horizons in Boulder, CO.

Written by Kent Odendahl for 5280 Magazine FACES of Denver 2018:

Lisa Marie utilizes a combination of Tibetan Buddhist principles, including Bodhicitta, along with the code of ethics for life coaching—a system that honors the client as an expert in their own lives. She utilizes Tarot cards for psychic readings and methodologies that have been used successfully for hundreds of years. "I want you to know you can heal yourself," she says. "You can get better. You can find love and happiness. I promise you, there is hope."

CPSIA information can be obtained
at www.ICGtesting.com
Printed in the USA
FSHW011330080119
54890FS